# TABLESAW SPECIALISTS

### Dead-Accurate Crosscut Sled
A simple sliding solution for conquering wide crosscuts.

Simply put, tablesaws are great ripping machines, but when it comes to crosscutting, a tablesaw miter gauge can't guide big boards as well as a crosscut sled. Unlike a miter gauge, a sled carries both halves of a workpiece past the blade. It allows you to safely and quickly make precision crosscuts while eliminating the chance of kickback.

This sled is designed to be as lightweight as possible without compromising strength or cutting accuracy. The ½"-thick base allows maximum blade height adjustment without being flimsy, and the fence and rail, which keep the sled flat and intact, are stepped down to reduce weight. A significant feature, the extension rail and quick-set stopblock allows for precise, efficient crosscutting of long work in multiples. You'll find that this jig completes your saw.

## NOTE

For accurate crosscutting, a saw table's slots must be parallel to the blade. If your saw needs adjustment, do it as described in your owner's manual before building the sled.

**FIGURE 1**

Crosscut Sled Exploded View

NOTE: For the items needed to make the sled, see the **Convenience-Plus Buying Guide** on page 9. Also, refer to the handy **Cut List** on page 9.

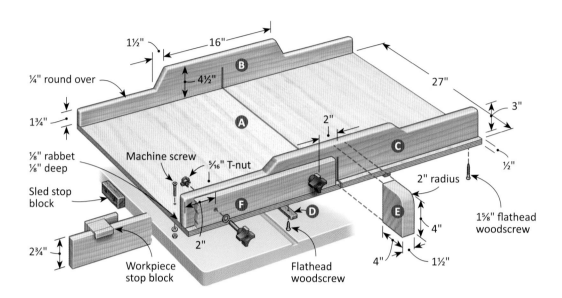

¼" round over

1½"

16"

4½"

B

27"

3"

1¾"

A

2"

C

½"

⅛" rabbet ⅛" deep

Machine screw

5⁄16" T-nut

2" radius

Sled stop block

F

D

E

4"

1⅝" flathead woodscrew

2¾"

Workpiece stop block

2"

Flathead woodscrew

4"

1½"

## Make the sled parts

**1** Saw the sled base (**Figure 1**, A) to size (refer to "Size the Sled to Suit Your Saw," below right). Orient the face veneer grain front to back as shown in **Figure 1**, so there will be no tear-out of the sled's saw kerf.

**2** Using a stable, straight-grained, moderately dense hardwood such as cherry, mahogany, or maple (I chose cherry), mill the boards for the rear rail (B) and fence (C). Joint and plane the fence to 1" thick, and the rail to ¾" thick. Make sure the edges are dead-straight and that the bottom of the fence is absolutely square to its faces. Cut the fence and rail to length to match your base (A).

**3** Saw or rout a ⅛ × ⅛" chip-clearance rabbet along the bottom inside face of the fence (C). This will prevent sawdust from impeding workpiece/fence contact.

**4** Referring to **Figure 1**, lay out the stepped shape of the rail (B) and fence (C), centering the humps over the blade location. Bandsaw the parts to shape, and then rout the top edges with a ¼" round-over bit for comfort.

**5** Using straight-grained maple or another dense hardwood, size the runners (D) to fit your saw's table slots snugly, but without side-to-side slop. To do this, thickness-plane a board until its edge barely slips into your slots, and then rip off a strip that's 1⁄16" narrower than the depth of the slots.

**6** Referring to the **Cut List** on page 9, make the blade guard (E), and then saw a 2" radius on one of its corners.

**WARNING:** The blade guard is not a handle. Do not use it to push the sled!

## SIZE THE SLED TO SUIT YOUR SAW

You'll need to size the width of the sled to suit your particular saw model. To determine your sled's side-to-side dimension, add 1½" to the distance between the blade and the left side of your table to create an overhang during assembly for easy fence adjustment. To that, add another 20" for the right-hand side of the fence. As for the front-to-back dimension, I recommend a 27" base, which will handle everything from small pieces up to 24"-wide panels (for cutting standard-depth base cabinet parts).

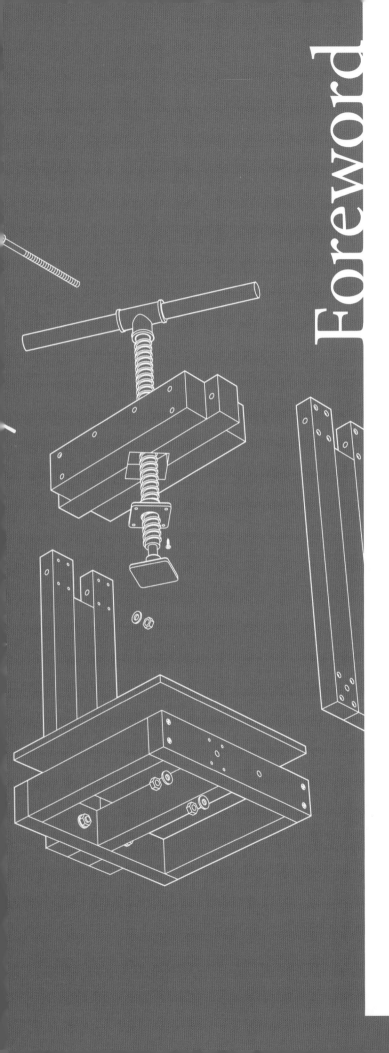

# HOME
## WOODWORKER
# SERIES

# Foreword

I f woodworkers are anything, they are problem solvers. When they encounter a tricky cut for a joint, need a level work support, or seek a safer and more precise way to perform a machining task, they come up with something that will work. But as you know, finding that something in the form of a helpful jig, fixture, or stand may take days of experimenting in the shop or hours of research poring through magazine back issues and books, or by exploring woodworking websites.

What if there were a book that contained a collection of plans for the most useful and popular types of jigs, fixtures, and stands for woodworking? Well, here it is! Part of the Home Woodworker Series, *Home Workshop Jigs and Fixtures* offers readers 46 projects to help them work better, smarter, faster, safer, and with greater precision than ever before. Indeed, this must-have book is your stepping stone to the next level of craftsmanship.

In it you'll find shop-proven plans to make your tablesaw, routers, and other machines do more. For your tablesaw alone, you'll find plans for a dead-accurate crosscut sled, a micro-adjustable box-joint jig, and a picture-framer's miter sled, to name a few.

Keeper jigs and guides abound for your routers as well. Among them are the slot-mortising jig, T-square and straightedge guides, and a jig for cutting clean, crisp dovetail slots for box making.

Also, be sure to check out the tricked-out drill-press table that lets you take on a wide range of challenges, including boring into the ends of project parts.

To add to the utility of your shop, consider building the adjustable assembly table that raises and lowers through the use of a car jack. And if you need a sturdy sawhorse or two, you'll find that *Home Workshop Jigs and Fixtures* includes three different styles, from easy-to-store versions to stout designs that offer handy storage underneath.

So there you have it, a hardworking book aimed at helping you solve any number of project-building and shop-related problems. Keep it close at hand, as you may find it the best friend a woodworker ever had.

—Jim Harrold, Editor

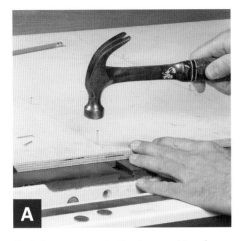

Tack the runners to the base with a few short nails. Leave the heads proud for easy removal later.

Attach the runners to the base with countersunk flathead screws.

## Attach the rail and runners

**1** Attach the rail (B) to the rear end of the sled base (A), countersinking 1⅝" flathead wood screws in from the underside. Make sure to drill screw clearance holes through the plywood to ensure the parts pull together securely.

**2** Place the runners (D) in the table slots, shimming them flush to the table surface using pennies. Lay the base (A) on top with its left edge overhanging the table by 1½". Register the saw's fence against the opposite edge to square the base to the table. Drive four or five 1" nails through the base into each runner to temporarily hold it in place (**Photo A**).

**3** Flip the base upside down and attach the runners using countersunk flathead screws that pass through screw clearance holes in the runners as shown in **Photo B**. Remove the nails.

**4** Flip the base upright and check its fit in the table slots. If the runners bind, use a card scraper or sandpaper block to take down the high spots. (To find the high spots, rub the inside edges of the table slots with a wide-lead carpenter's pencil; then push the sled back and forth. Any graphite on the runners indicates areas that need trimming.)

## Outfit and install the fence

**1** Lay out the T-nut locations on the fence (C), where shown in **Figure 1**, that will be used for connecting the extension rail (F). *(Note: If you prefer feeding workpieces from the right-hand side, insert the T-nuts on that side of the fence.)*

**2** Using a 1"-diameter Forstner or multi-spur bit on the drill press, drill a ¹³⁄₁₆"-deep counterbore at each location. Next, drill a through-hole to accommodate the T-nut sleeve and install the nuts.

**3** Raise the tablesaw blade about 1½" above the table and saw the sled kerf, stopping about 6" from the trailing end of the base. Remove the sled, set the fence (C) ¾" in from the front edge, and attach it from underneath with a single 1⅝" screw at the far right end.

**4** Unplug your saw. Place the sled back in the table slots. Clamp a hefty jointed board to the fence to remove any slight bow, which can cause out-of-square cuts. Raise the blade to full height, square the fence to it, and clamp the left-hand end of the fence to the base as shown in **Photo C**.

Pivot the fence so that it's square to the blade and clamp it to the base. The jointed board clamped to the fence removes any slight bow.

**D**

Make a test crosscut using a long, wide board with parallel edges. Afterward, flip one-half over (Part B in the inset) and butt the two ends together. When they meet perfectly, the fence is dead-square to the blade.

**E**

Glue the long-grain edge of the blade guard to the fence, ensuring that it's square to the base.

**5** Using a wide piece of scrap with absolutely parallel edges, make a test crosscut (**Photo D**). Now flip one of the halves over and butt it against the other. If the sawn ends don't meet perfectly along their entire length, adjust the fence angle and try again until there is no gap between the two (**Photo D inset**).

**6** With the fence and stiffener board still tightly clamped in place, screw the fence to the base. Space the screws roughly 6" apart. Make sure to drill screw clearance holes so the parts pull together tightly.

### Install the guard and sled stop

**1** Attach the blade guard (E), gluing its long-grain edge to the fence. Make sure that it's square to the base, as it serves as registration for the end of the extension rail (**Photo E**).

**2** For safety, the sled should stop when the top of the blade meets the inside face of the fence. To ensure this, insert a countersunk flathead machine screw into the overhanging section of the base as shown in **Figure 1**. Then bolt a mating stopblock for it to the side of your saw table. (If you use an outfeed table, simply make its miter gauge slots short enough to stop the sled at the proper point.)

### Make the extension rail and stopblock

**1** Rip a piece of ¾"-thick stock to 2¾" wide to make the extension rail (**Figure 1**, F). Crosscut it to the length that serves the kind of work you do. (Mine is 60" long.)

**2** To mark the knob hole locations on the rail (F), make a drill guide by boring a ¼"-diameter hole through the edge of a 1"-wide squarely dressed scrap block, using the drill press.

**3** Butt the extension rail (F) against the blade guard (E) and clamp it to the sled fence. Insert a ¼" brad-point drill bit through the drill guide and a T-nut. Holding the guide firmly, turn the bit by hand to mark the hole center in the rail (**Photo F**).

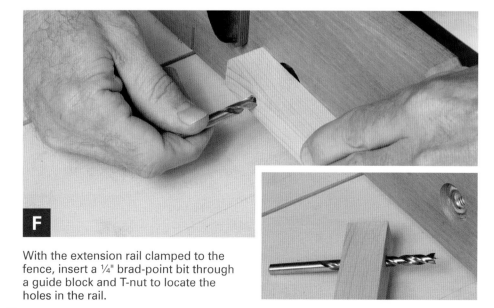

**F**

With the extension rail clamped to the fence, insert a ¼" brad-point bit through a guide block and T-nut to locate the holes in the rail.

For cutting long boards accurately, attach the extension rail to the fence and use the stopblock.

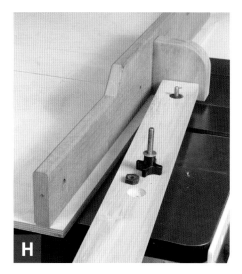

Shop-made rubber washers keep the knobs attached when the rail is detached from the sled.

**4** Drill the ⁵⁄₁₆"-diameter knob stem holes in the extension rail (F) using the drill press. Attach the rail to the fence using the four-arm knobs (**Photo G**). To avoid losing the knobs, counterbore the inside face of the rail to accommodate rubber O-rings or similar keepers (**Photo H**).

**5** Starting with stock at least 12" long (enough to mill safely), make the stopblock front (G), core (H), and retaining strip (I) to the dimensions in the **Cut List** and as shown in **Figure 2**, **Stopblock Detail**. As you glue the three pieces together, make sure that all the faces and edges are square to each other.

**6** Wax the underside of the sled and the runners to allow for smooth sliding action. No finish is needed.

## FIGURE 2
### Stopblock Detail

## Convenience-Plus Buying Guide

## Crosscut Sled Cut List

| | PART | THICKNESS | WIDTH | LENGTH | QTY. | *MAT'L |
|---|---|---|---|---|---|---|
| A | Base | ½" | Suit saw* | 27" | 1 | BBP |
| B | Rear rail | ¾" | 4½" | * | 1 | C |
| C | Fence | 1" | 4½" | * | 1 | C |
| D | Runner | Suit saw** | Suit saw** | 27" | 2 | M |
| E | Blade guard | 1½" | 4" | 4" | 1 | C |
| F | Extension rail | ¾" | 2¾" | varies | 1 | C |
| G | Stopblock front | ¼" | 3" | 4" | 1 | C |
| H | Stopblock core | 1¹³⁄₁₆" | 3" | 2½" | 1 | C |
| I | Stopblock retaining strip | ½" | ¾" | 2½" | 1 | C |

**Materials:** C=Cherry, M=Maple, BBP=Baltic Birch Plywood
\*   See "Size the Sled to Suit Your Saw," page 6.
\*\*   See "Make the sled parts," page 6.

## Crosscut Sled Support Arm
### Taming tilt at the tablesaw.

The only problem with a large crosscut sled is that it tends to tip off the front of the saw when pulled backward to load a wide panel. You can use an auxiliary stand for support, but a less intrusive approach is to craft a short support arm that cantilevers off the front of the saw.

Like many woodworkers, I have a Biesemeyer fence. I've found that a simple three-piece wooden support attaches nicely to it. The support consists of a wooden arm that lays across the fence's guide tube while dadoed into a crosspiece that fits snugly between the fence tube and the fence mounting rail. A cleat on the inside face of the crosspiece presses against the underside of the tablesaw wing, locking the unit in place. The unit installs and removes in a flash and can be modified to fit many similar saw/fence combinations.

Make the crosspiece about 16" long and just thick enough to slide snugly between the fence tube and its mounting rail. If necessary, round over the bottom edge to seat the piece against the face and bottom of the L-shaped mounting rail. Trim the top edge to sit just a hair below the table top; then cut a 3"-wide dado whose bottom sits flush with the top of the fence tube (**Photo A**). Locate the dado about 6" in from the outer end of the crosspiece. Make the 12"-long support arm to fit snugly in the dado (**Photo B**), but don't fasten it yet.

Next, make the cleat that bears against the underside of the saw. Mine is ⅞ × 2½ × 11", but suit your particular tablesaw wing, ensuring that the cleat bears solidly against its underside edge. Notch the long edge to accommodate the fence mounting rail, with 4" or 5" solidly contacting the wooden crosspiece (**Photo C**). Holding the cleat in place, mark its location on the crosspiece (**Photo D**). Finally, glue and screw the parts together and radius the corners of the arm.

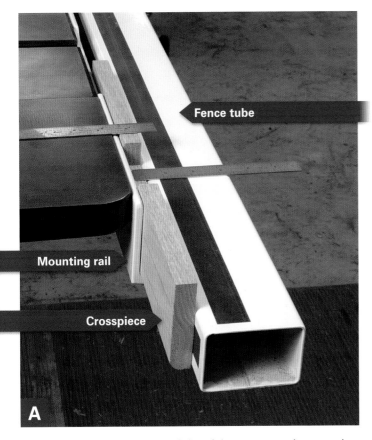

**Fence tube**

**Mounting rail**

**Crosspiece**

**A**

Use small rulers or short, straight sticks to ensure the top edge of the crosspiece sits flush to the saw table, and the dado bottom aligns with the fence tube.

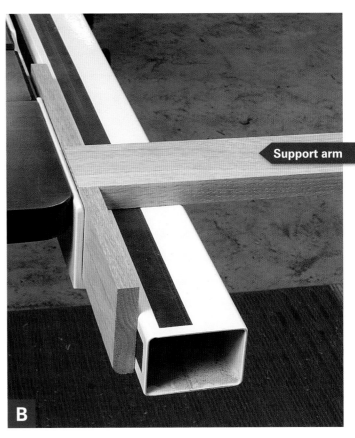

**Support arm**

**B**

Thickness the support arm so that its top face is flush with the top edge of the crosspiece while resting on the fence tube.

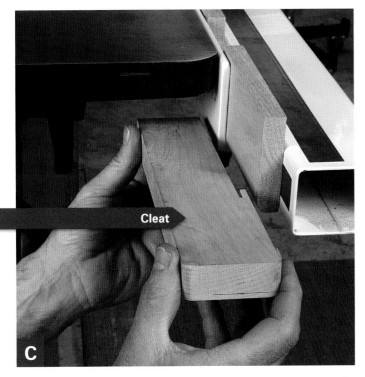

**Cleat**

**C**

Notch the cleat to snugly wrap around the fence mounting rail while firmly contacting the inside face of the crosspiece.

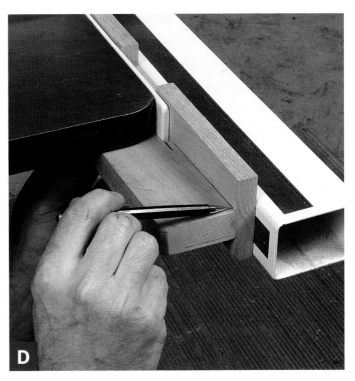

**D**

Hold the cleat firmly against the underside of the saw wing; mark its position on the face of the centerpiece.

## Tablesaw Tapering Jig
A simple sliding sled for making legs safely.

Using a tablesaw to cut tapered legs isn't rocket science, but some jigs make the job a lot harder than it needs to be. Those simple hinge-bar tapering jigs are awkward to use. Trying to hold the blank against the jig and keep the jig against the fence while making the cut is too much of a struggle.

This sled-style tapering jig makes the process safe and nearly foolproof. Adjustable cams allow for exact positioning to match cutlines, and shop-made aluminum hold-downs prevent the work from shifting in mid-cut. A runner attached to the underside of the base ensures that the jig and workpiece slide smoothly and safely past the blade. Last but not least, a comfortable plane-style handle helps keep fingers away from the saw blade.

Note that the jig in these photos is a bit different than the one shown in the drawing. I made my jig from parts on hand. The drawing shows an improved version made from readily available materials (see the **Convenience-Plus Buying Guide** on page 14).

### Make the parts
The base needs to be rigid and sturdy, but thin enough to enable the saw blade to cut through thick stock. I used ½"-thick pre-painted Ready-To-Go (RTG) plywood, but Baltic birch would also work.

**1** Using a tablesaw, cut the base (A), blanks for the cams (B), and the stopblock (C) to size. Round the sharp corners of the base as shown in **Figure 1**, using a bandsaw or disc sander. Then rout a ¼" round-over on both faces, with the exception of the edge that will abut the blade.

**2** Make two full-sized copies of the **Cam Pattern** (see **Online Extra** at left) and affix them to your cam blanks. Saw the cams to shape, sand the profiles, and then soften the edges on both faces with a ¼" round-over bit.

**3** On the underside of the base, lay out the holes as indicated in **Figure 1**. Along the inner row, drill ⅝"-diameter × ¼"-deep counterbores, for the bolt heads. Next, use a ¼"-diameter bit to bore the through holes for the bolts. Drill the ¼" holes in the stopblock (C), and ¼" and ¼" holes in the cams (B). Countersink the pivot hole in each cam so that its screwhead sits flush.

## ONLINE EXTRA

For full-sized patterns of the cams, hold-downs and handle, go to woodcraftmagazine.com/onlineextras.

FIGURE 1

NOTE: For the items needed to make the sled, see the **Convenience-Plus Buying Guide** on page 14. Also, refer to the handy **Cut List** on page 14.

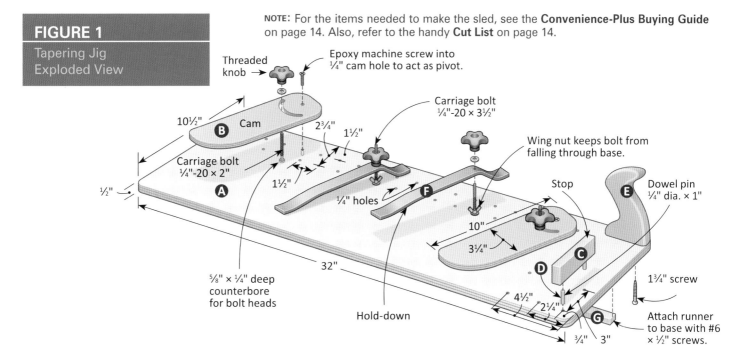

Threaded knob →

Epoxy machine screw into ¼" cam hole to act as pivot.

10½"

**B** Cam

2¾"

1½"

Carriage bolt ¼"-20 × 3½"

Wing nut keeps bolt from falling through base.

Carriage bolt ¼"-20 × 2"

**A**

½"

1½"

¼" holes

**F**

Stop

**E**

Dowel pin ¼" dia. × 1"

10"

3¼"

**C**

⅝" × ¼" deep counterbore for bolt heads

32"

Hold-down

**D**

4½"

2¼"

1¾" screw

¾"   3"

**G**

Attach runner to base with #6 × ½" screws.

**4** Cut two dowel pins (D) to peg the stopblock (C) to the base (A). Epoxy the machine screws into the cams (B) to serve as pivots, and the dowel pins into the stopblock (C).

**5** Using ½"-thick plywood or MDF, make the **Cam-Slotting Jig** shown in **Figure 2**. Chuck a 15⁄16" straight bit into your table-mounted router and position the base so that the bit is centered in the ⅜" cam hole as shown. Clamp the base to the router table, and then rout the slots in both cams.

**6** Download the full-sized **Handle Pattern** (see **Online Extra**, page 12) and affix it to a scrap of hardwood. Saw the handle (E) to shape and sand to your line. Round over the front and back edges as needed to make a comfortable grip.

**7** Using a hacksaw, cut the aluminum stock to length to make the hold-downs (F). Drill the 5⁄16" hole where shown on the **Hold-Down Pattern** download (see **Online Extra**, page 12). Now use a metal-jawed vise to bend the stock to shape. The finished shape doesn't need to be perfect, but don't overlook the little dip at the front end. The small flat is needed to apply pressure to the blank.

**8** Size the runner (G) to fit your saw's miter gauge slot. Place the runner in the slot, shimming it flush to the table's surface if necessary. Lay base (A) on top so that the left edge is the thickness of matchbook cardboard from the blade. Position your rip fence against the right side of the base to ensure that it's parallel to the blade. (Note: Some woodworkers prefer positioning the edge of the base against the blade to create an exact reference. Setting the base my way leaves extra material for removing burns or saw marks.)

**9** Drive a few 1" nails through the base into the runner to temporarily secure it. Flip the base upside down, attach the runner with countersunk flathead screws, and then remove the nails.

**10** Screw the handle (E) to the base (A). Wax the runner and underside of the base, and you're ready to put your new jig to work.

FIGURE 2

Adjust base to position bit in starting hole, and then pivot cam as shown to rout slot.

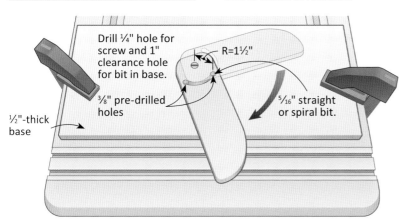

Drill ¼" hole for screw and 1" clearance hole for bit in base.

R=1½"

⅜" pre-drilled holes

5⁄16" straight or spiral bit.

½"-thick base

## Tapering Jig Cut List

| | PART | THICKNESS | WIDTH | LENGTH | QTY. | MAT'L |
|---|---|---|---|---|---|---|
| A | Base | ½" | 10½" | 32" | 1 | BBP |
| B | Cams | ½" | 3¼" | 10" | 2 | BBP |
| C | Stopblock | ½" | 1" | 4¼" | 1 | BBP |
| D | Dowel pins | ¼" dia. | | 1" | 2 | M |
| E | Handle | ¾" | 2¾" | 4⅝" | 2 | Any Hardwood |
| F | Hold-downs | ¼" | 1" | 10" | 2 | Aluminum |
| G | Runner | Suit saw | Suit saw | 32" | 1 | M |

**Materials:** BBP=Baltic Birch Plywood; M=Maple
**Hardware:** (2) ¼"-20 × ¾" flathead machine screws, (4) #6 × ½" flathead wood screws,
(2) #8 × 1¾" flathead wood screws, (2) ¼"-20 × 2" carriage bolts,
(2) ¼"-20 × 3½" carriage bolts, (4) ¼" flat washers, (2) ¼"-20 wing nuts

## Convenience-Plus Buying Guide

## USING THE TAPERING JIG

Here's how to saw a classic two-sided tapered leg. The process—marking, clamping, and cutting—doesn't take much longer than reading about it. Two notes before you begin: First, mortise your leg stock before you taper, since mortising is easier on square stock. Second, consider your cut sequence beforehand. Make the two cuts in an order that allows uncut faces to reference against your stops and base. Otherwise, you'll need to reset your jig or stabilize the tapered face using the offcut wedge.

**1** Lay out the leg. Mark out the finished foot on the bottom of the leg, and the location of the apron on the top.

**2** Position the leg on the jig, aligning the marks you made across the foot and face with the edge of the jig. Abut the top of the leg against the stopblock, and secure the leg with one hold-down. Adjust the cams to fine-tune the leg's position, and then tighten the second hold-down. Make sure that the aluminum won't contact the saw blade.

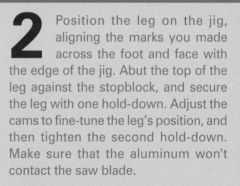

**3** After making the first cut, turn off the saw, rotate the leg, and make the second cut.

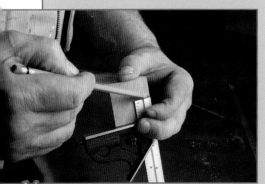

**OVERALL DIMENSIONS | 18¼"w × 12"d × 4¼"h**

## Micro-Adjustable Box-Joint Jig
Make projects with a choice of four finger sizes.

**B**ox joints provide a strong, attractive way to assemble drawers, chests, and boxes of all types. But to cut clean, consistent fingers and notches you need a jig that adjusts in fine increments. Unlike the tablesaw jigs that cut only one size finger, this model, with its switchable finger keys, lets you cut precision box joints having ⅛", ¼", ⅜", or ½" fingers. After micro-adjusting the setting with the end knob, you can lock it in with the two five-star knobs. Also, the replaceable hardboard backers eliminate tear-out, resulting in splinter-free cuts.

### First, make the jig

**1** From ¾" stock, cut the fixed fence (A) and adjustable fence (B) to the sizes in the **Cut List**. Mill stock to ½" thick, and cut the fence end (C) and blade cover (D) to size. Mill stock to ¼" thick, and cut the fixed base (E), four key bases (F), and the miter slot runner (G). The runner should fit your saw's slot with no slop and be 1⁄16" above the tabletop.

**2** Drill ¼" blade start holes and rout the 1½" slots in the fixed fence (A) where shown in **Figure 1**, page 16.

**3** Chuck a ½" × 14° dovetail bit in a table-mounted router. Now raise it for a ¼"-deep cut for the 2¼"-wide dovetailed recess in the adjustable fence (B) in **Figure 1**. Adjust

the router-table fence, and make a cut along one cutline. Adjust the fence again, and cut along the second cutline as shown in **Photo A**, page 16. Continue adjusting the fence and remove the waste between these two cuts. Finally, angle-cut the chamfers at the ends of the fence.

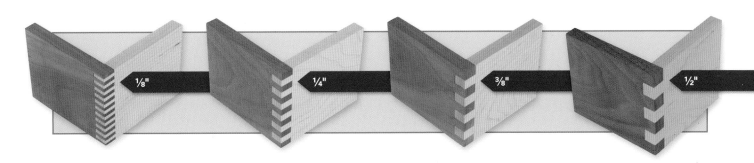

⅛"    ¼"    ⅜"    ½"

## FIGURE 1
Box-Joint Jig Exploded View

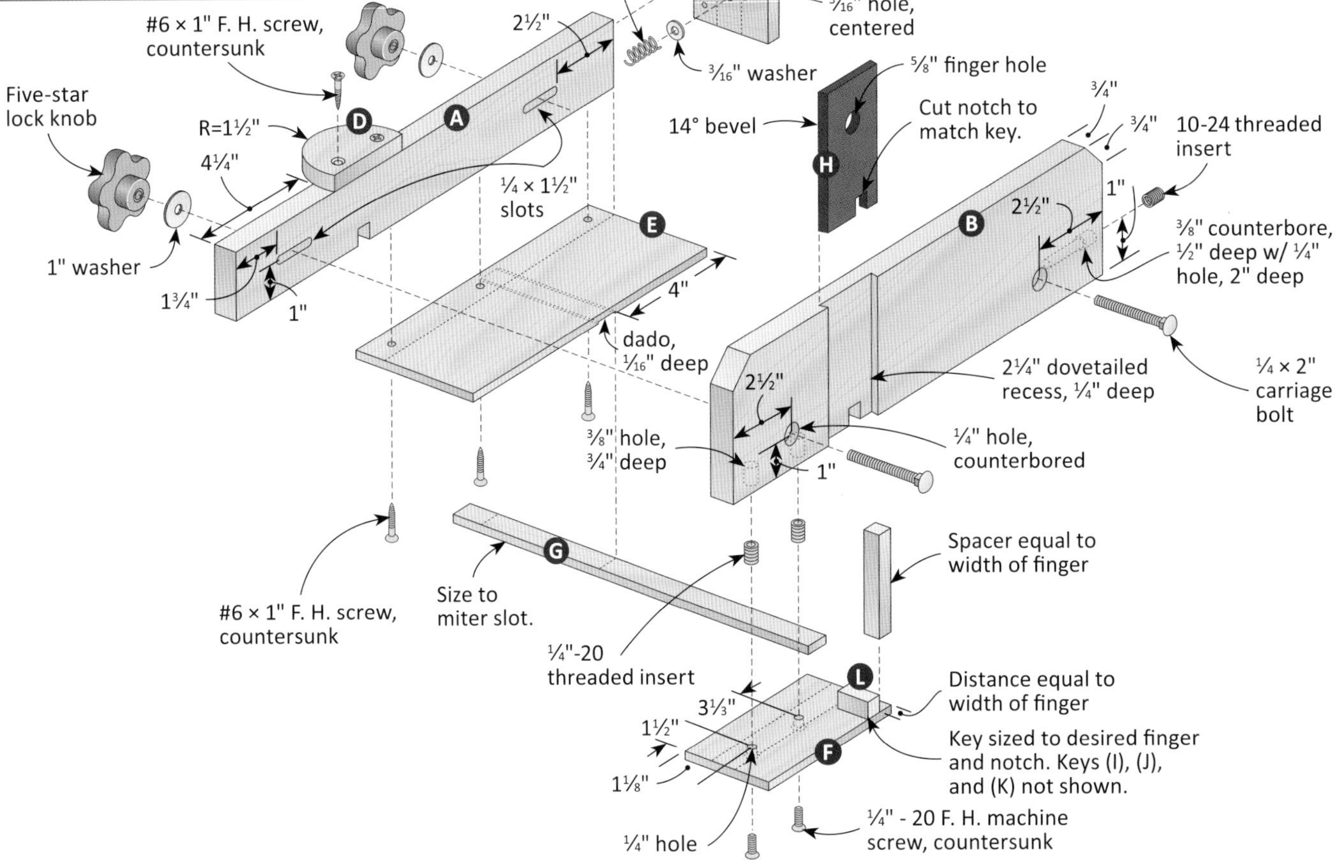

#6 × 1" F. H. screw
½" wood mushroom knob w/ ½"-deep centered hole
3/16 × 2 ½" all-thread
Spring
C
3/16" hole, centered
#6 × 1" F. H. screw, countersunk
2½"
3/16" washer
⅝" finger hole
Five-star lock knob
R=1½"
D
A
14° bevel
Cut notch to match key.
¾"
¾"
10-24 threaded insert
4¼"
H
¼ × 1½" slots
E
1"
B
2½"
⅜" counterbore, ½" deep w/ ¼" hole, 2" deep
1" washer
1¾"
1"
4"
dado, 1/16" deep
2½"
2¼" dovetailed recess, ¼" deep
¼ × 2" carriage bolt
⅜" hole, ¾" deep
¼" hole, counterbored
1"
Spacer equal to width of finger
G
#6 × 1" F. H. screw, countersunk
Size to miter slot.
¼"-20 threaded insert
L
Distance equal to width of finger
3⅓"
1½"
F
Key sized to desired finger and notch. Keys (I), (J), and (K) not shown.
1⅛"
¼" hole
¼" - 20 F. H. machine screw, countersunk


**4** Measure the width of the dovetailed recess in **Step 3** in the adjustable fence (B), and cut a 24" strip of ¼" hardboard to this width. Rout 14° bevels along the edges of the strip with the same dovetail bit. Test-fit the strip in the recess. If it fits, crosscut the backers (H) to final length. (Consider cutting a batch of backers for later use.)

**5** Switch to a straight bit sized to your miter slot runner (G), or, using a dado set, cut the 1/16"-deep dado in the bottom face of the fixed base (E). Test-fit the runner in the dado. Glue it in place.

**6** Lay out and bandsaw the blade cover (D) to shape, sanding the edges smooth.

**7** Lay out the screw and threaded insert hole locations, referencing **Figure 1**. Now bore the holes, countersinking where indicated.

**8** Carefully cut ⅛"-, ¼"-, ⅜"-, and ½"-square 12"-long strips for keys (I), (J), (K), and (L) and the spacer stock, measuring the strips' thickness as shown in **Photo B**. Also check the stock for square. Now cut the keys to length, and glue them one key width from the inside end of the adjustable key bases (F). Finally, cut 3"-long pieces from each strip of key stock to serve as setup spacers and label them.

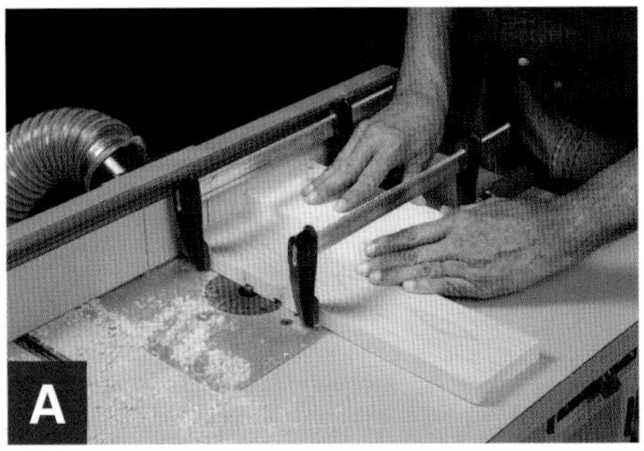

A


Clamp on a sacrificial pushblock to rout the dovetailed recess in the adjustable fence to avoid tear-out.

**9** With the hardware shown in **Figure 1**, assemble the jig parts. Widen the hole in the wooden knob for the all-thread rod if needed, and epoxy the knob to the rod. You're now ready to put the jig to work.

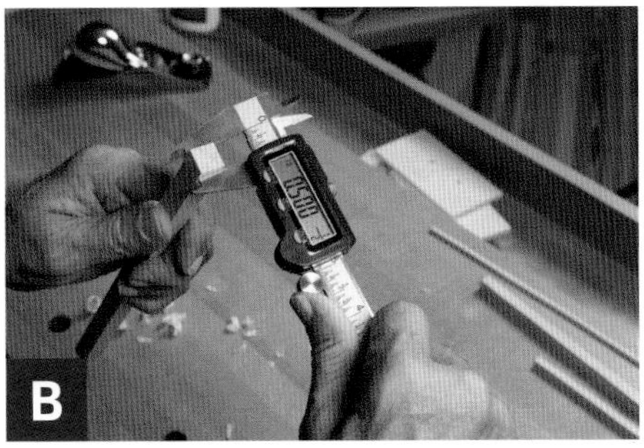

B


Establish dead-on key and spacer stock with a caliper; reduce the thickness with sanding or planing.

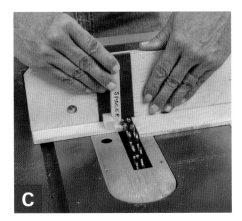

**C**

Use the spacer to fix the distance between the key and dado set, adjusting the key with the knob.

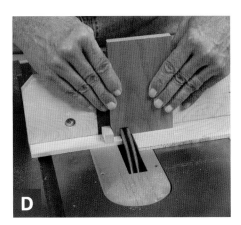

**D**

Holding the workpiece snug to the adjusted key, move the jig forward and make the first cut.

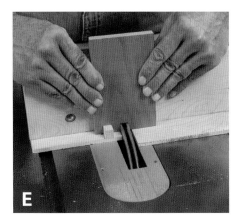

**E**

Straddling the key with the workpiece, cut the remaining fingers and notches.

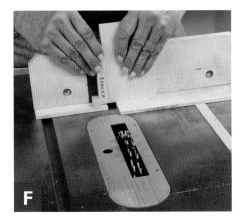

**F**

Use the spacer to determine the corner or beginning notch on the mating workpiece.

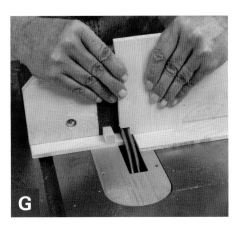

**G**

With the spacing of the mating workpiece established, cut the corner notch.

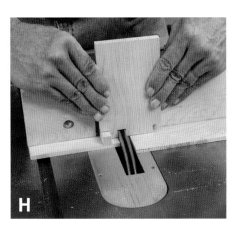

**H**

Place the corner notch on the key and cut the next finger and notch. Cut out the remaining notches.

## Put the jig to work

**1** Based on the desired finger and notch widths (I chose ½"), install a matching dado set and key base (F). Make a test cut in scrap, and fit the appropriate spacer in the notch. Add shims to the dado set to ensure a perfect fit. Now raise the dado set to a height equal to the combined thickness of your workpiece and fixed base. (For ½" stock, I raised the dado set to ¾".)

**2** Set the jig against the front edge of the dado set. With the correct spacer (M) held against the key on the key base (F), turn the wooden adjustment knob until the spacer just grazes the dado set (**Photo C**). Tighten the five-star lock knobs.

**3** Using stock the same thickness as the project parts, set one "test" workpiece against the key and make the cut (**Photo D**).

**4** Place the first test workpiece notch over the key, and make the second notch cut (**Photo E**). Continue cutting the remaining fingers and notches across the width.

## BOX-JOINT POINTERS

- For good-looking corners, adjust the width of the sides to be an increment of the finger.
- Joints that terminate with full fingers are preferred over joints that terminate with one notch and one finger.
- While you can cut box side widths when cutting the lengths, some woodworkers cut widths proud by ⅛" to ½", trimming the assembled box to final width.
- Cut the notches at both ends of one workpiece first and those on same-length workpieces before cutting the neighboring notches.
- For box bottoms, rout stopped grooves instead of through grooves to avoid creating unsightly joints.

**5** Place the spacer (M) against the key and the mating test workpiece against it to establish the corner notch location (**Photo F**).

**6** Clasp or clamp the workpiece firmly to the fence so it doesn't move, and remove the spacer. Cut the notched corner on the mating test piece (**Photo G**).

**7** Place the corner notch over the key, and cut the fingers and remaining notches (**Photo H**). Fit the mating test pieces together. To fine-tune the joint, see **Figure 2** and cut another pair of mating sides. For design help, see **Box-Joint Pointers**, page 17. Now cut your project parts.

## Convenience-Plus Buying Guide

- ☐ 1 Whiteside Dovetail Bit, ½" D × 14° (½" SH)
- ☐ 2 Five-Star Knob w/Through Hole, ¼"-20, 2 needed
- ☐ 3 Lauréy Wood Mushroom Knob, 1½"
- ☐ 4 Brass Insert, ¼"-20, 10/pkg.
- ☐ 5 Brass Insert, #10-24, 10/pkg.
- ☐ 6 Freud 8" Pro Dado Set

### FIGURE 2
Fast Fixes for Faulty Joints

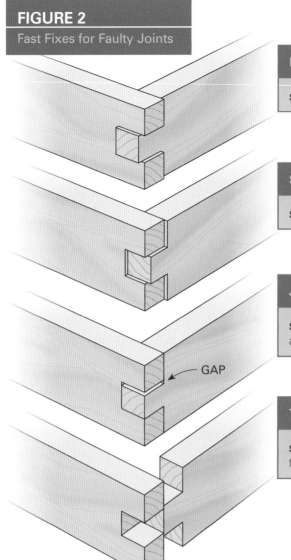

**Proud Fingers**

SOLUTION: Lower the dado set.

**Shy Fingers**

SOLUTION: Raise the dado set.

**Joint Gaps**

SOLUTION: Micro-adjust key away from the blade.

— GAP

**Thick Fingers**

SOLUTION: Micro-adjust key toward the blade.

## Box-Joint Jig Cut List

| | PART | THICKNESS | WIDTH | LENGTH | QTY. | MAT'L |
|---|---|---|---|---|---|---|
| A | Fixed fence | ¾" | 2" | 16½" | 1 | M |
| B | Adjustable fence | ¾" | 4" | 16" | 1 | M |
| C | Fence end | ½" | 2" | 2½" | 1 | M |
| D* | Blade cover | ½" | 2" | 3" | 1 | M |
| E | Fixed base | ¼" | 4" | 10¼" | 1 | M |
| F | Key bases | ¼" | 2⅝" | 5³⁄₁₆" | 4 | M |
| G** | Miter slot runner | ⅜" | ¾" | 12" | 1 | M |
| H | Backers | ¼" | 2¼" | 1" | 4 | TP |
| I | ⅛" key | ⅜" | ⅛" | 1" | 1 | M |
| J | ¼" key | ¼" | ¼" | 1" | 1 | M |
| K | ⅜" key | ⅜" | ⅜" | 1" | 1 | M |
| L | ½" key | ½" | ½" | 1" | 1 | M |
| | Spacer | same as key | same as key | 3" | 1 | M |

**Materials:** M=Maple, TP=Tempered Hardboard
**Hardware:** (1) ³⁄₁₆ × 2½" all-thread rod; (1) ⅜" × 1" steel spring; (1) ³⁄₁₆" washer; (2) ¼ × 2" carriage bolts; (2) ¼" washers; (5) #6 × 1" flathead screws; (2) ¼ × ¾" flathead machine screws.
\* Indicates parts are initially cut oversized. See instructions.
\*\* Size runner to saw's slot.

## Picture-Framer's Miter Sled
Achieve frame-shop perfection.

A key to creating perfectly mitered picture frames and similar items is this useful jig. It will result in the tightest possible joints, ensuring that your craftsmanship displays just as well as the images you frame.

**A**

Gripping frame sides to the jig's sandpaper edge, miter-cut the left ends.

**B**

From the rabbet's *inside* corner at the mitered end, mark the cutline at the opposite end of the frame side.

Adjust the stop. Then, holding the workpiece in place, trim it to final length.

**1** To build the sled, cut the rail and base to the sizes and shapes shown. Before adding the triangular lamination to the base, mark a centerline on the base from the front to back edge. Set the base on the saw table, align the centerline with the saw blade, slide the fence over, and lock it in place.

**2** Now, remove the base. Place washers in the miter slots and set a pair of Incra miter sliders on the washers. The washers should elevate the sliders just above the table. Add double-faced tape to the tops of the slides, and then carefully lower the base on them and against the fence. Flush the trailing edge of the sled with the ends of the slides. With the slides adhered to the base, mark the screw and adjustment screw holes and drill them. Attach the slides and set the sled base on the saw. Using an Allen wrench, adjust the slides so that there's no slop; then raise the blade 1" and cut one-third into the base.

**3** Next, make a 1½"-thick lamination, and cut it to a perfect 18 × 18" square. Cut the rabbet along one edge for the Incra T-Track Plus stop system and install it. Then bore the 1" handle hole. Make the stop as shown in the **Stop Details** and set it aside.

**4** Using double-faced tape, set the lamination on the base with one corner centered on the saw kerf, and adjacent corners equidistant from the trailing edge. Raise the saw blade and check that the angle between the lamination's edges and blade measures 45°. Flip the base and screw the lamination in place. Adhere sandpaper to the lamination's right edge. (You could also add sandpaper to the left edge if cutting long moldings.) Cut and glue in the dowel handle.

## FIGURE 1
### Tablesaw Miter Sled

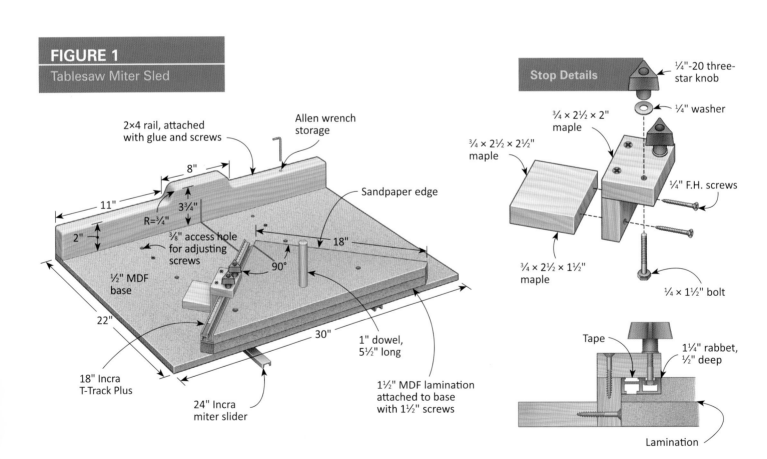

**5** Now, remove the slides, turn the sled 90°, and trim off the protruding part of the lamination flush with the trailing edge of the base. Replace the slides. Raise the blade, and make a cut into the lamination's corner, stopping at 3". This cut snips off the aluminum track where it intersects with the cutline, exposing the rabbet beneath.

**6** Finally, ensure the blade is exactly at 90° to the table. Then, using the sled, miter-cut two pieces of scrap of the same width, one from the right edge and one from the left edge of the lamination. Hold the mitered ends together in the cradle of a square. If a fine crack appears horizontally, sand the miters slightly until they meet snugly at both the inside and outside corners. If the pieces fail to meet vertically, tweak the angle of your saw blade. Test-cut again.

## To Build Your Frames

**1** Build the tablesaw miter sled in **Figure 1,** using the accompanying instructions.

**2** Study the cutting sequence in **Figure 2** for the best grain match. Then, working from the lengths for your short and long frame sides, crosscut the molding stock to size plus ⅛", labeling each piece. Now, miter-cut the left ends of the frame sides (**Photo A**, page 19).

**3** Using your rabbet opening dimensions, lay out the cutline on the right-hand end of one long side, as shown in **Photo B**, page 19. Note that the rabbet opening dimensions should be ⅛" longer and wider than the glass, photo, mat board, and back for clearance. The rabbet opening for an 8" × 10" photo, for instance, should measure 8⅛ × 10⅛", unless it receives a mat board surround and requires a larger frame.

**4** Place the workpiece on the sled and set up the stop, aligning the cutline with the kerf. Lock the stop, and make the cut, as shown in **Photo C**, page 20. Cut the remaining long side. Adjust the stop, and repeat for cutting the short sides. Note the stop's scale location on the T-track for future frames.

**5** Dry-assemble the frame sides on a flat surface, and check the fit. While an accurate sled guarantees a tight joint, if you need to touch up the cut ends, rub them on disc sander disc a few times with the tool off, using a miter gauge set at 45°.

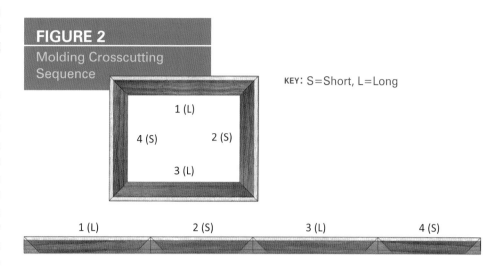

**FIGURE 2**
Molding Crosscutting Sequence

**KEY:** S=Short, L=Long

1 (L)

4 (S)   2 (S)

3 (L)

1 (L)   2 (S)   3 (L)   4 (S)

Stop

Hold-down

## Box-Maker's Miter Sled
Keeper jigs make this construction spot-on accurate and repeatable.

**M**akers of decorative boxes forever seek novel ways to join box sides and present a special look using favorite—often figured—woods and other materials. They also want box-making jigs to speed the cutting and assembly assignments and for achieving perfection. Here's a super-accurate box-maker's miter sled to add to your box-making arsenal.

**1** Cut the base and machine the dadoes and rabbet.

**2** Radius the front corners, and cut the T-tracks to length. Drill ½" holes in the tracks to accept the cap screws. Epoxy the tracks in place.

**3** From dressed hardwood, cut the fence and stiffener. Cut the groove in the fence, round over the corners on both pieces, and screw them in place. Cut and screw in the fence T-track.

**4** Cut the blade guard from face-joined stock. Center it on the fence, and glue it in place.

**5** Make the stop.

**6** Install the miter slider hardware, using package instructions. Add the hold-downs and stop.

### TIP ALERT

I used ¾" phenolic-faced MultiPly for its stability and smooth-gliding surfaces. If you have flat, quality plywood handy in the shop, use it to save on cost.

## FIGURE 1
### Box-Maker's Miter Sled

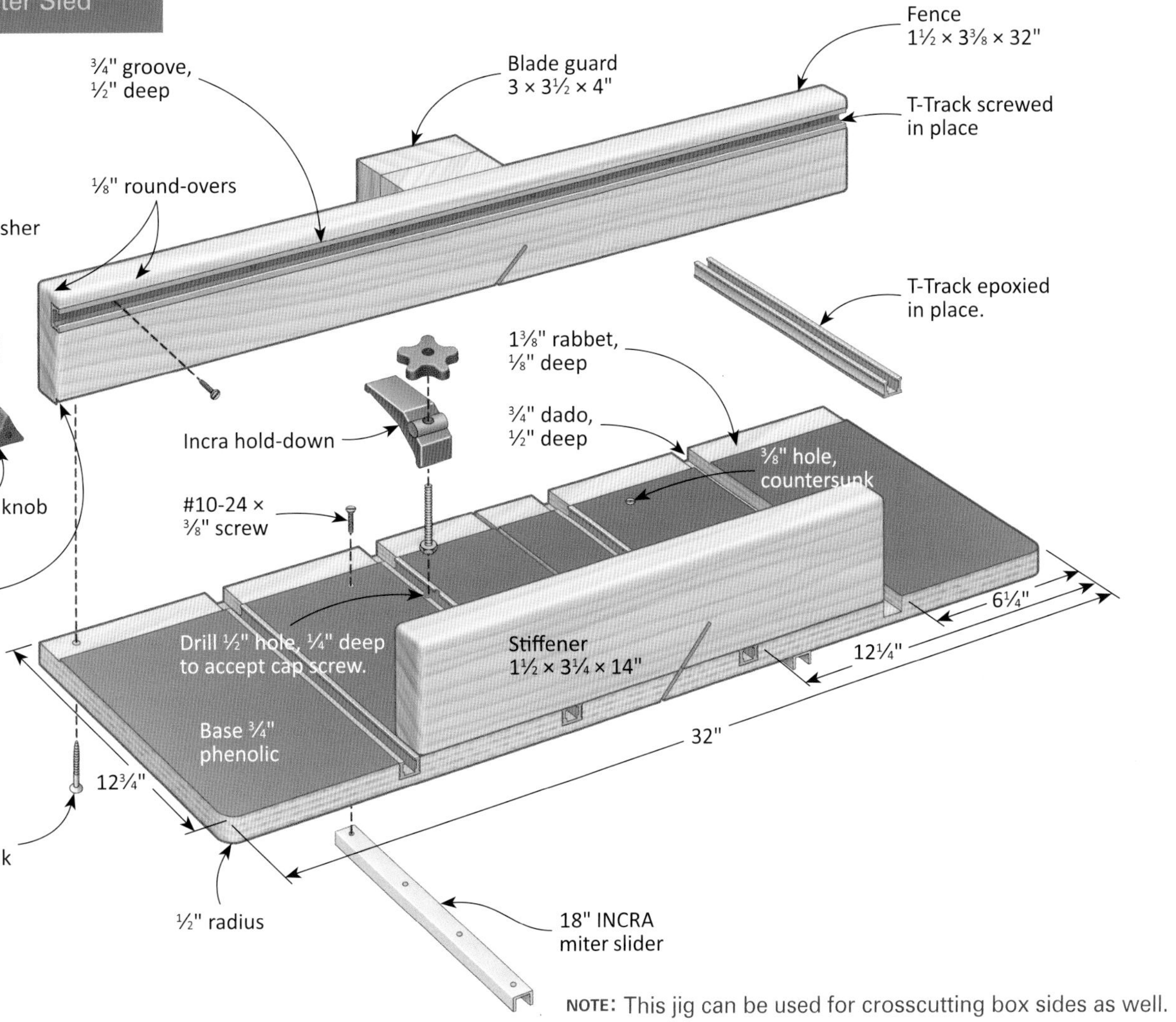

Fence
$1\frac{1}{2} \times 3\frac{3}{8} \times 32"$

Blade guard
$3 \times 3\frac{1}{2} \times 4"$

$\frac{3}{4}"$ groove,
$\frac{1}{2}"$ deep

T-Track screwed
in place

$\frac{1}{8}"$ round-overs

$\frac{1}{4}\text{-}20 \times 1\frac{1}{2}"$
cap screws

$\frac{5}{16}"$ washer

T-Track epoxied
in place.

$1\frac{3}{8}"$ rabbet,
$\frac{1}{8}"$ deep

$\frac{3}{4}"$ dado,
$\frac{1}{2}"$ deep

Incra hold-down

$\frac{3}{8}"$ hole,
countersunk

Stop
$\frac{3}{4} \times 2\frac{1}{2} \times 3\frac{1}{4}"$

$\frac{1}{4}\text{-}20$ knob

$\frac{1}{4}"$ rabbet, $\frac{1}{8}"$ deep
for dust chute

#10-24 ×
$\frac{3}{8}"$ screw

$6\frac{1}{4}"$

Drill $\frac{1}{2}"$ hole, $\frac{1}{4}"$ deep
to accept cap screw.

Stiffener
$1\frac{1}{2} \times 3\frac{1}{4} \times 14"$

$12\frac{1}{4}"$

Base $\frac{3}{4}"$
phenolic

32"

#8 × $2\frac{1}{2}"$ flathead
screw, countersunk

$12\frac{3}{4}"$

$\frac{1}{2}"$ radius

18" INCRA
miter slider

**NOTE:** This jig can be used for crosscutting box sides as well.

# Convenience-Plus
# Buying Guide

| | |
|---|---|
| ☐ 1 | Phenolic Faced MultiPly, $\frac{3}{4} \times 24 \times 48"$ |
| ☐ 2 | Incra T-Track, 24", qty. 2 |
| ☐ 3 | Incra T-Track, 36" |
| ☐ 4 | Incra Aluminum Miter Slider, 18", qty. 2 |
| ☐ 5 | Incra Build-It Knob Kit, $\frac{1}{4}\text{-}20$, 8 sets/pkg. |
| ☐ 6 | Incra Hold-Down Clamp, qty. 2 |
| ☐ 7 | System Three 5-Minute Epoxy, $\frac{1}{2}$ pt. |

## Thin-Stock Hold Down Jig
### Keep your workpiece flat on the table.

Not knowing what to do with the MagJigs is likely the biggest challenge manufacturer Magswitch has in selling the items. Consequently, the company spent time developing jigs that are well suited for the MagJigs. We borrowed them to give you two practical shop applications, complete with dimensions.

This clever thin-stock hold down jig is made from one piece of solid wood and consists of four graduated steps for holding down ⅛"-, ¼"-, ⅜"-, and ½"-thick stock.

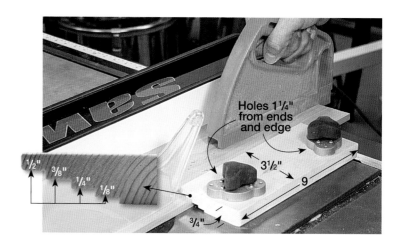

Holes 1¼" from ends and edge

½"  ⅜"  ¼"  ⅛"

3½"

9

¾"

## Cove Molding and Dado Guide System
### Control your workpiece during tricky cuts.

Employing a pair of stock-containing scrapwood guides, this jig includes two MagJigs in each opposing guide strip, as well as a T-track, and a Magswitch vertical featherboard (#147528).

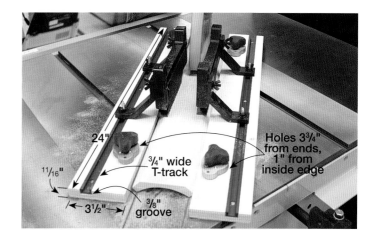

24"

11/16"

3/4" wide T-track

3/8" groove

3½"

Holes 3¾" from ends, 1" from inside edge

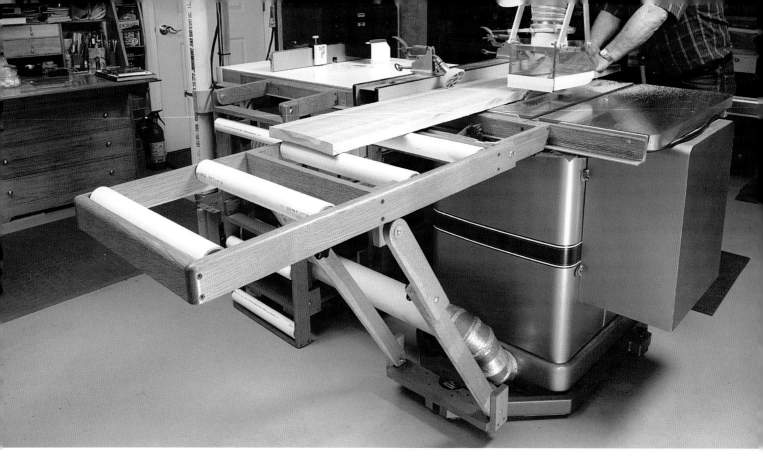

## Adjustable Outfeed Rollers
### Simplicity and efficiency.

The rollers are made from 1½" PVC pipe. Cut plugs from ¾" stock and drill ¼" holes for axles. Then use a disk sander on each blank, sanding just enough of a taper so it will fit inside the pipe. The frame shown here is oak; the rollers are 16" long. With a 35"-high table top, make each section 34" long, allowing for an inch of floor clearance.

**FIGURE 1**
Adjustable Outfeed Rollers

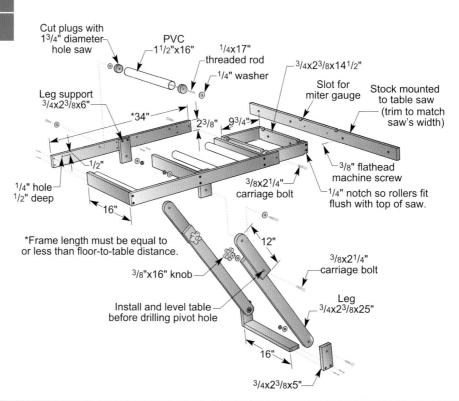

Cut plugs with 1³/4" diameter hole saw

PVC 1¹/2"x16"

¹/4x17" threaded rod

¹/4" washer

³/4x2³/8x14¹/2"

Slot for miter gauge

Stock mounted to table saw (trim to match saw's width)

Leg support ³/4x2³/8x6"

*34"

2³/8"

9³/4"

1/2"

³/8" flathead machine screw

¹/4" hole ¹/2" deep

³/8x2¹/4" carriage bolt

¹/4" notch so rollers fit flush with top of saw.

16"

*Frame length must be equal to or less than floor-to-table distance.

12"

³/8"x16" knob

³/8x2¹/4" carriage bolt

Leg ³/4x2³/8x25"

Install and level table before drilling pivot hole

16"

³/4x2³/8x5"

The toggle clamps in the spline-cutting jig immobilize the frame for a clean cut while keeping your hands safely away from the blade.

## Spline-Slot Jig
### Easily reinforce corners with splines.

Make the spline-cutting jig by following the figure. Many table saw blades have an alternate top bevel (ATB) grind that produces a kerf bottom shaped like an inverted V. This would result in objectionable gaps when you insert the spline. To avoid this gap, choose a blade that has a square-topped tooth, such as an ATBR grind or one made for a flat bottom kerf. Another option is to use one of the side blades from a stack dado set. Cut the spline slots into each frame corner as shown in the photo.

### FIGURE 1
Spline-Slot Jig

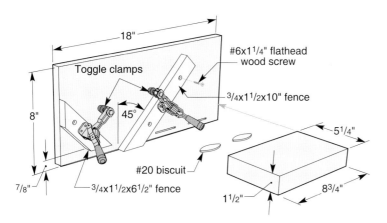

- 18"
- Toggle clamps
- #6x1¹/₄" flathead wood screw
- ³/₄x1¹/₂x10" fence
- 45°
- 8"
- 5¹/₄"
- #20 biscuit
- 7/8"
- ³/₄x1¹/₂x6¹/₂" fence
- 1¹/₂"
- 8³/₄"

# CHAPTER 2
# MAKING ROUTERS DO MORE

### Slot-Mortising Jig
Rout ends and edges accurately with this rail-guided jig.

Some woodworkers discount loose tenons as the poor machine-cut cousin of traditional mortise-and-tenon joinery, but I've found the joint useful in many instances. Joining parts using a pair of matching mortises and a snug-fitting wood strip, instead of sawing a tenon to fit a mortise, saves stock. And with the proper setup, loose tenon joinery is just as strong as its competition, but quicker and easier to accomplish.

Wanting a slot mortiser but not willing to spend money for a commercial model, I used leftover material and spare hardware to create a simple rail-guided mortising jig for my plunge router. Despite my initial success, I further improved the jig by adding Bessey's auto-adjust toggle clamps. Now my revised jig is just as reliable and accurate as its predecessor, but thanks to the new toggles, slippage is a thing of the past. Once set, the auto-adjust hold-downs provide the same amount of pressure on a 2½"-thick leg as on a ¾" rail without needing to adjust the footpad.

The jig can hold stock up to 8" wide and 3¾" thick. By adjusting the base dimensions, you can easily mortise still larger parts.

OVERALL DIMENSIONS | 18"w × 5¾"d × 10"h

**FIGURE 1**
Base Exploded View
and Base Elevations

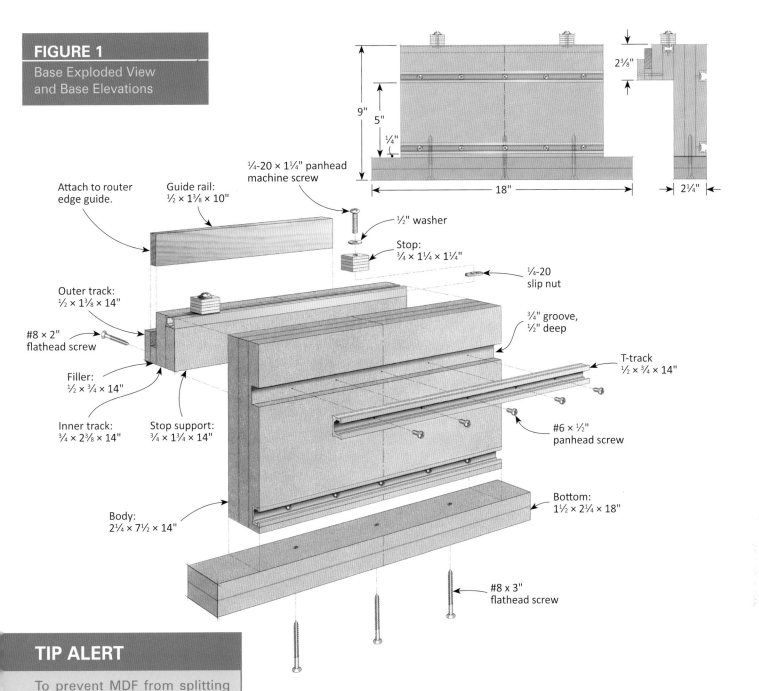

Attach to router edge guide.

Guide rail:
½ × 1⅜ × 10"

¼-20 × 1¼" panhead machine screw

½" washer

Stop:
¾ × 1¼ × 1¼"

¼-20 slip nut

Outer track:
½ × 1⅜ × 14"

#8 × 2" flathead screw

¾" groove, ½" deep

T-track
½ × ¾ × 14"

Filler:
½ × ¾ × 14"

#6 × ½" panhead screw

Inner track:
¾ × 2⅜ × 14"

Stop support:
¾ × 1¾ × 14"

Body:
2¼ × 7½ × 14"

Bottom:
1½ × 2¼ × 18"

#8 x 3" flathead screw

9"
5"
¼"
18"
2⅜"
2¼"

## Build the base

**1** As shown in **Figure 1**, make the base in sections, starting with the body. From ¾"-thick MDF, cut three pieces slightly larger than the finished dimensions. Laminate the pieces together, and then trim an edge and end to correct an uneven edge and slice away any squeeze-out. Now trim the uncut edge and end to final dimensions. Cut two ½"-deep dadoes across the front face, where shown, to fit the T-track.

**2** From ¾"-thick MDF, cut the stop support and inner track. Glue the stop support to the body, where shown. Use a piece of T-track to ensure that the installed track will be flush with the jig's top edge. Let the glue cure, and then attach the inner track, again using T-track to ensure that the jig's top edge is flush.

**3** From ½"-thick MDF, cut the filler and outer track to size. Glue the two together, and then attach them to the inner track with glue and 2" screws. Wipe away any squeeze-out, especially in the groove for the guide rail.

**4** To make the bottom section, start with two oversized pieces of ¾"-thick MDF, glue and clamp the stack together, and then trim to final dimension. Drill clearance holes where shown, and then attach with glue and 3"-long screws. Make sure that the front edge of the bottom is flush with the jig's face.

**5** Using a hacksaw, cut the T-track into three 14"-long sections, and attach them to the assembled base, where shown, with ½"-long screws.

**6** Cut the stops from ¾" plywood, drill holes, and attach to the top T-track, as shown.

**7** Plane a strip of hardwood to fit within the outer and inner tracks to serve as the rail for your router's edge guide. Finally, draw a centerline across the top and front face of the jig.

## Build the end fence and hold-downs

**1** Laminate ½"-thick plywood to make the 1"-thick mortising fence and clamp bases. Trim the fence and bases to size, referring to **Figure 2**. Lay out the location for the bolt and screw holes used to secure the fence and clamp bases to the face of the jig. To mark the screw holes needed to attach the clamps, position the clamps on the plywood, and transfer the hole locations.

Using a drill press, drill ¼" and ³⁄₁₆" clearance holes where marked. Counterbore the screw holes so that the heads sit just below the face of the plywood.

**2** Rip two ⁵⁄₁₆ × ³⁄₈" guide strips, and attach them to the bottom of the clamp bases. (The strips keep the clamps aligned even when the slip nuts aren't cinched tight.)

**3** Attach the auto-adjust clamps to the fence and clamp bases.

## FIGURE 2
Mortising Fences

**End Mortising**

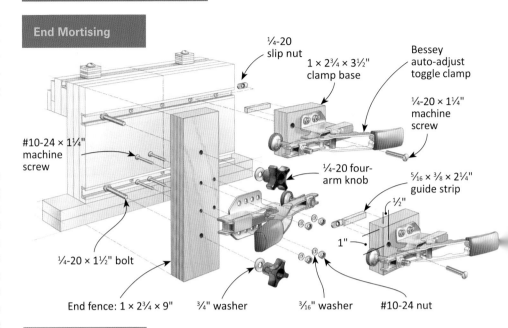

¼-20 slip nut
1 × 2¾ × 3½" clamp base
Bessey auto-adjust toggle clamp
¼-20 × 1¼" machine screw
#10-24 × 1¼" machine screw
¼-20 four-arm knob
⁵⁄₁₆ × ³⁄₈ × 2¼" guide strip
½"
1"
¼-20 × 1½" bolt
End fence: 1 × 2¾ × 9"
¾" washer
³⁄₁₆" washer
#10-24 nut

**Edge Mortising**

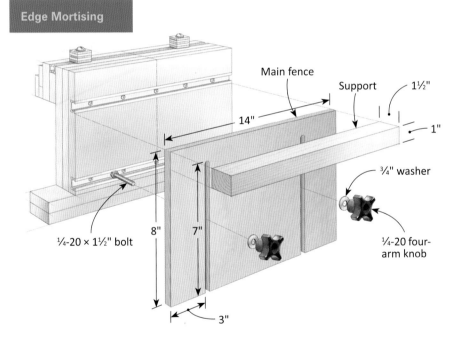

Main fence
Support
1½"
14"
1"
¾" washer
8"
7"
¼-20 × 1½" bolt
3"
¼-20 four-arm knob

## Build the edge fence

**1** From ¾"-thick plywood, cut the main fence to the size shown in **Figure 2**. Lay out a pair of ¼"-wide slots, as shown.

**2** Using a drill press, drill a ¼"-diameter hole at the top edge of each slot layout. Next, rout the slots using your router table and a ¼"-diameter straight bit.

**3** Rip a strip of 1"-thick hardwood to 1½" wide, and then cut it to 14" long. Glue it to the top edge of your main fence. This strip can serve as an edge for clamping smaller stock or as a support for a longer board, for instance, when mortising the edges of legs or longer stock.

## Using the jig

Routing mortises is simple. These instructions will ensure consistent results. First, lay out the mortises. Even if you intend to mortise across the center of your stock, always register your layout tools against the outside (show) face of your workpiece. Draw or scribe a line to indicate the center of your mortise. Next, mark a perpendicular line across the center of the width to position the parts on the jig.

Outfit your router with an appropriate bit (I prefer an upcut spiral), and attach the rail to your router's edge guide.

To set up the jig for end routing, first clamp the jig to your workbench, as shown. Use a clamping base to temporarily register the workpiece in the jig, to align the mortise layout with the jig's centerline. Next, set the mortising fence against the opposite edge, remove the board, and use a square to set the fence perpendicular to the top edge of the jig. Cinch the knobs to secure the fence in place.

Now, clamp the board to the fence, making sure that the end of the workpiece is flush with the top of the jig. Slide the clamp bases against the opposite edge of the work, tighten the locking screws, and engage the toggles.

Adjust your router's edge guide to center the bit on the mortise layout. Set the stops on the top of the jig to match the mortise length.

To rout, plunge the router to full depth at each end of the mortise (**Photo A**). To finish up, work from end to end, plunging in ¼" increments.

For making edge mortises, replace the end fence with the edge fence. Set the fence so that the top edge of the workpiece is flush with the jig's top face. Align the centerline on the workpiece with the jig, and clamp in place. Lock the stops in their appropriate positions, and rout the mortise (**Photo B**).

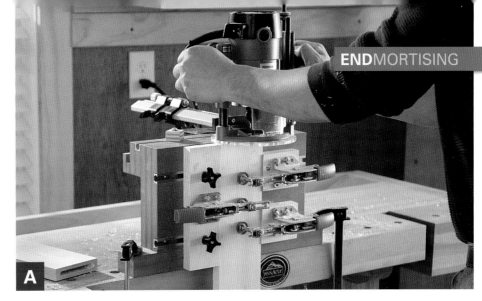

ENDMORTISING

Rout the mortise in ¼"-deep increments to avoid overtaxing the router or bit. The trio of auto-adjust hold-downs offers solid support when routing end grain.

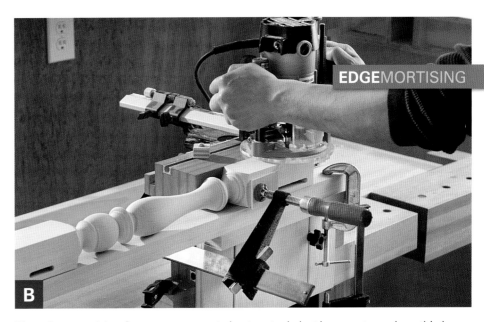

EDGEMORTISING

The edge-mortising fence can support shorter stock, but long parts such as this leg may require additional support.

To make your tenons, plane hardwood stock to fit the slot, rip to width, and then round the edges with a round-over bit or file to fit the mortise. Crosscut the tenon stock ¹⁄₁₆" shorter than needed to allow room for glue.

Apply glue to the loose tenon, slide it into one mortise and attach the mating part. Once the glue dries, nobody will know how it was assembled because no one will be able to pull it apart.

## Convenience-Plus Buying Guide

| | |
|---|---|
| ☐ 1 | Incra T-Track 48" |
| ☐ 2 | Bessey Auto-Adjust Horizontal Toggle Clamps, qty. 3 |
| ☐ 3 | Four-Arm Knob With ¼-20 Insert, qty. 2 |
| ☐ 4 | Sliding T- (slip) nut ¼-20, qty. 4 |

## TIP ALERT

To ensure that the mortises line up, always clamp the "show" face of your parts against the face of the jig.

## Box-Maker's Dovetail Slot Jig
Rout crisp, perfect openings for dovetail keys.

Makers of decorative boxes forever seek novel ways to join box sides. They also want box-making jigs to speed the cutting and assembly assignments and for achieving perfection. Here's a router-table dovetail slot jig that fills the bill.

Stop

Hold-down

Straightedge

With the box aligned and secured with hold-downs, move the jig along the fence to cut a clean, splinter-free dovetail slot.

## FIGURE 1
### Dovetail Slot Jig

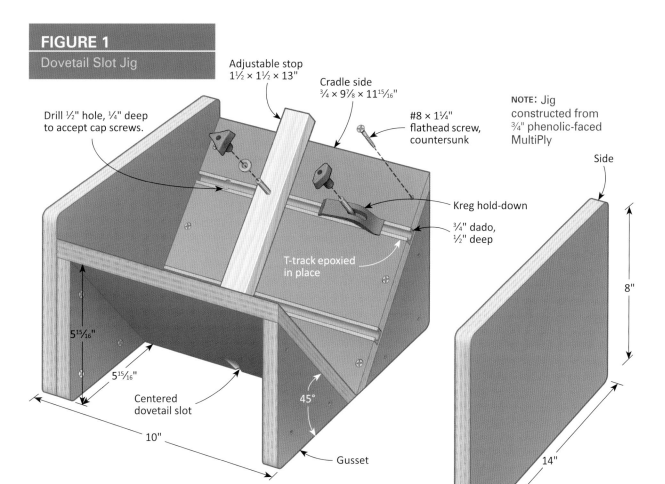

Drill ½" hole, ¼" deep to accept cap screws.

Adjustable stop
1½ × 1½ × 13"

Cradle side
¾ × 9⅞ × 11¹⁵⁄₁₆"

#8 × 1¼"
flathead screw,
countersunk

NOTE: Jig
constructed from
¾" phenolic-faced
MultiPly

Side

Kreg hold-down

¾" dado,
½" deep

T-track epoxied
in place

5¹⁵⁄₁₆"

5¹⁵⁄₁₆"

Centered
dovetail slot

45°

10"

Gusset

8"

14"

**1** Cut the sides, gussets, and cradle sides, bevel-cutting the latter where shown. Cut and sand the radii on the sides and gussets.

**2** Rout two dadoes for the T-track in the top face of one cradle side. Cut two T-tracks to length, and use a twist bit to drill shallow ½" holes at one end of each track to accept the cap screws. Epoxy in place.

**3** Drill countersunk pilot holes, and screw the cradle sides to the gussets. Screw the gussets to the sides.

**4** Drill countersunk pilot holes, and screw the gussets to the sides.

**5** Cut the adjustable stop, and drill the knob hardware holes.

**6** Add the hold-downs and stop to the jig.

## Convenience-Plus Buying Guide

| | | |
|---|---|---|
| ☐ | 1 | Phenolic Faced MultiPly, ¾ × 24 × 48" |
| ☐ | 2 | Incra T-Track, 24" |
| ☐ | 3 | Incra Build-It Knob Kit, ¼-20, 8 sets/pkg. |
| ☐ | 4 | Kreg Track Clamp, qty. 2 |
| ☐ | 5 | System Three 5-Minute Epoxy, ½ pt. |

¼-20 × 2½"
cap screws

¼-20 knob

**Adjustable Stop Detail**

⁵⁄₁₆" washer

½"

¾"

T-Track

Squeeze the shelf material between the sacrificial guides (Inset) to set the dado width. Factor in the guide thickness when setting bit depth.

## T-Square and Straightedge
Make precise rabbets, dadoes, and grooves.

Straightedge and T-square guides rank as two of the simplest jigs going, offering great versatility when paired with a router. Both work well for rabbets, dadoes and grooves. You can also use them for neatly trimming the ends of plywood panels or wide glued-ups too large to cut on a tablesaw. Working in tandem, these guides can help you make measure-free dadoes (see photo, above.)

Make the straightedge portion of your jig from a straight board about 6 inches longer than the material you expect to rout. (If you're making the T-square guide, rip a second shorter strip and attach it to one end. Drive one screw then check the angle with a carpenter's square to set the fence before driving the remaining fasteners.)

Add the width of your straightedge to the bit-to-base edge distance of your router and rip a slightly oversized strip of ⅛" thick Marlite or hardboard. Attach the strip to the straightedge with double-faced tape.

Finally, trim the ⅛" bottom with your router and straight bit.

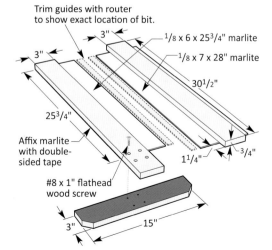

Trim guides with router to show exact location of bit.

3"

3"

⅛ x 6 x 25¾" marlite

⅛ x 7 x 28" marlite

30½"

25¾"

Affix marlite with double-sided tape

1¼"

¾"

#8 x 1" flathead wood screw

3"

15"

## Breadboard Jig
Rout tongues that fit.

The breadboard jig isn't that different from the straightedge, but the row of 1" diameter holes along the bar enables you to align the top and bottom fence so that you can rabbet both faces of a large panel for making the wide tenons found in breadboard ends. Make the jig as shown about a foot longer than you might typically need; three dowel pins provide better alignment than two.

Starting with a strip of 1½" thick by 4" wide maple (6/4 oak or a kiln-dried two-by stock would also work), joint and plane the faces and edges, and then drill a line of alignment holes where shown in the figure. Rip the blank in half then attach the guides with double-faced tape.

To set the jig, position the panel between the dowels, align the sacrificial guide with the shoulder line, and clamp it together. Rout the top face of the workpiece, and then flip the assembly and workpiece to finish the opposite face. Test the fit of the tongue before removing the jig.

## FIGURE 1
Breadboard Jig

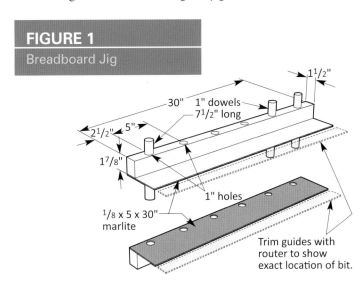

1½"

30" 1" dowels
7½" long

2½" 5"

1⁷/₈"

1" holes

¹/₈ x 5 x 30" marlite

Trim guides with router to show exact location of bit.

## Two-Faced Straightedge
### For ripping and jointing.

I f you think using a flush-trim bit with a straightedge in lieu of a jointer isn't new, then check out this jig's flip side. Outfitting it with two 48"-long miter channels enables it to work with track-saw-style clamps so that you can setup your workpiece as needed, and then do your ripping and jointing on a pair of sawhorses or at your bench.

You can build this back-saving jig from a few strips of ½"-thick MDF or plywood. Rabbet the jointer-edge so that the aluminum angle rests flush with the surface. Make the ripping guide strip wider than the blade-to-base dimension of your circular saw so that the first cut sets the cut line. Screw the guide strip to the assembly so that you can replace it if you change saw blades.

To put the jig in jointer mode, simply flip it over and position the stock so that the edge hangs over the aluminum angle. Routing edges with a flush-trim helical bit produces an edge as clean as you'd expect from a well-tuned jointer. Carbide should be used on materials that would quickly dull high-speed knives, such as melamine, MDF, and plywood.

### FIGURE 1
Two-Faced Straightedge

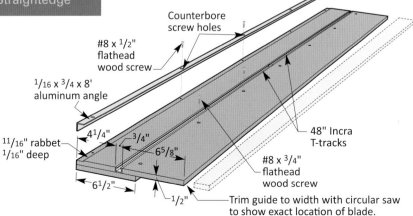

Counterbore screw holes

#8 x ¹/₂" flathead wood screw

¹/₁₆ x ³/₄ x 8' aluminum angle

4¹/₄"

³/₄"

6⁵/₈"

¹¹/₁₆" rabbet ¹/₁₆" deep

6¹/₂"

¹/₂"

48" Incra T-tracks

#8 x ³/₄" flathead wood screw

Trim guide to width with circular saw to show exact location of blade.

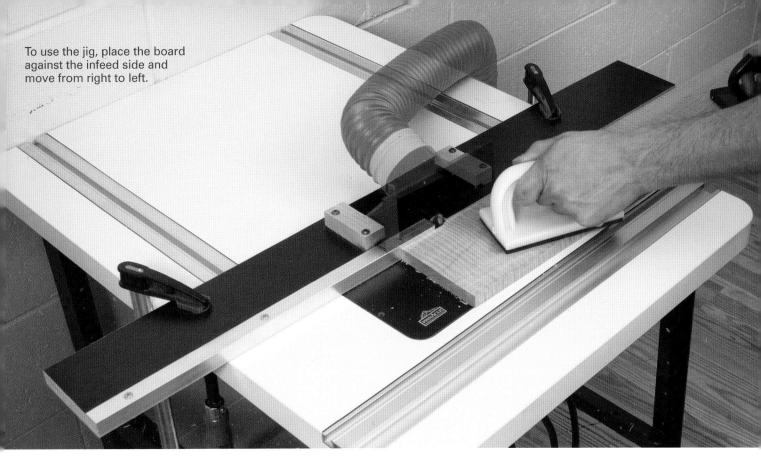

To use the jig, place the board against the infeed side and move from right to left.

## Router-Table Jointer Fence
Trim true edges for edge-joining.

This table-mounted router jig offers a safe way to joint boards that might be too short to safely machine on a standard jointer. And since spiral or helical bits cause less tear-out than straight jointer knives, you're likely to save stock when working figured woods.

Two-cut settings make this jig different. It can rout a heavier $1/16$"-deep cut for regular jointing, and a super-light cut equal to the thickness of plastic laminate (about $1/32$") for difficult materials.

To set up the jig, clamp one end to your router table. Use a straightedge to position the fence so the outfeed fence is tangent to the circumference of the bit, then clamp the remaining free end.

### FIGURE 1
Jointer Fence

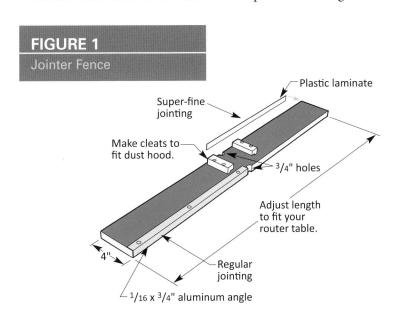

Plastic laminate

Super-fine jointing

Make cleats to fit dust hood.

$3/4$" holes

Adjust length to fit your router table.

4"

Regular jointing

$1/16$ x $3/4$" aluminum angle

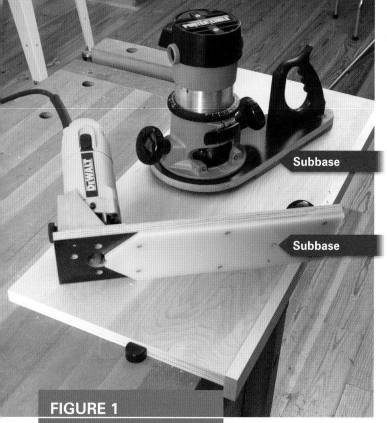

Subbase

Subbase

## FIGURE 1
Full-Sized Baseplate

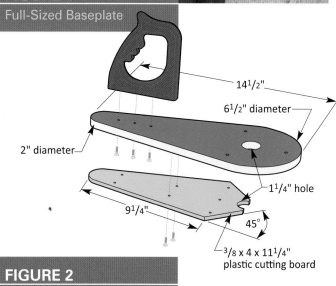

14¹/₂"

6¹/₂" diameter

2" diameter

1¹/₄" hole

9¹/₄"

45°

³/₈ x 4 x 11¹/₄"
plastic cutting board

## FIGURE 2
Trimmer-Sized Baseplate

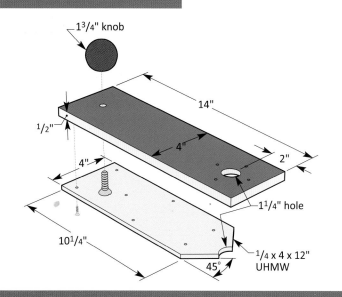

1³/₄" knob

14"

¹/₂"

4"

4"

2"

1¹/₄" hole

10¹/₄"

45°

¹/₄ x 4 x 12"
UHMW

These offset base plates add stability to edge-routing.

Use the two-level base to quickly and cleanly cut solid wood banding level with the a plywood face panel.

## Full-Sized and Trimmer-Sized Baseplate
Flush-trim work edges with more control.

Removing the subbase transforms the jig into an offset base. Apply a little weight on the handled end to keep the router from tipping.

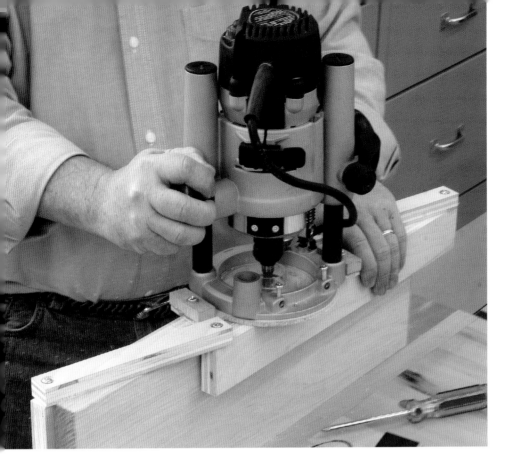

## Self-Centering Slot-Cutting Jig

Mortise slots in edges in short order.

Finding the exact center for routing slots in the edge of a workpiece just got a whole lot easier with this scrapwood project. Here, the arms pivot, collapsing the sides against the workpiece, making quick work of mortising slots with a handheld plunge router. Size the circular base to match the base of your tool.

### FIGURE 1
Self-Centering
Slot-Cutting Jig

Washer

#8 x 1¼"
panhead screw

1"

8"

⅛" plywood

#8 x 1¼"
panhead screw

¾" counterbore
¾" deep with
a screw hole
centered inside

½ x ¾ x 2"

2"

¾" plywood

8"

17"

2"

**NOTE:** Use clamps to secure jig to work in order to hold router with both hands.

## Flush-Trim Handheld Router Jig
### Tackle edge work on large panels with ease.

To save time and achieve perfect results when applying edge banding to plywood, create this simple flush-trim jig for your trim router. It consists of scrap materials from the shop and an acrylic baseplate to which the trim router mounts. When in use, the adjustable carriage rests on the surface of the edged workpiece and glides along as shown. The baseplate acts as a fence, keeping the jig snug to the edge for the flush-trimming duration. At outside corners, add a temporary sacrificial block to the shelf being trimmed, holding it in place with double-faced tape. This allows the bit's bearing to go beyond the corner.

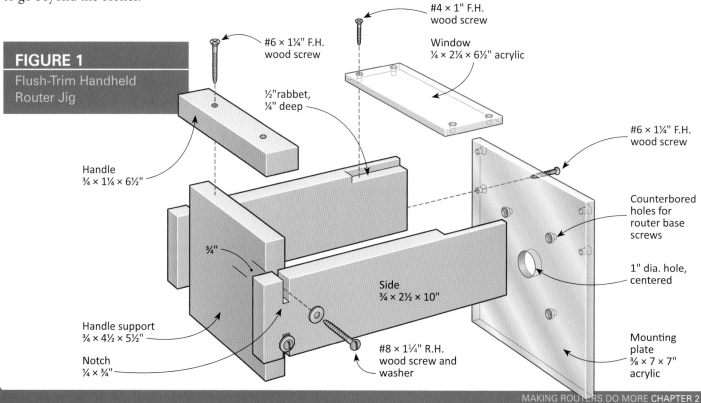

**FIGURE 1**
Flush-Trim Handheld
Router Jig

#4 × 1" F.H.
wood screw

#6 × 1¼" F.H.
wood screw

Window
¼ × 2¼ × 6½" acrylic

½"rabbet,
¼" deep

Handle
¾ × 1¼ × 6½"

#6 × 1¼" F.H.
wood screw

Counterbored
holes for
router base
screws

¾"

1" dia. hole,
centered

Side
¾ × 2½ × 10"

Handle support
¾ × 4½ × 5½"

Notch
¼ × ¾"

#8 × 1¼" R.H.
wood screw and
washer

Mounting
plate
⅜ × 7 × 7"
acrylic

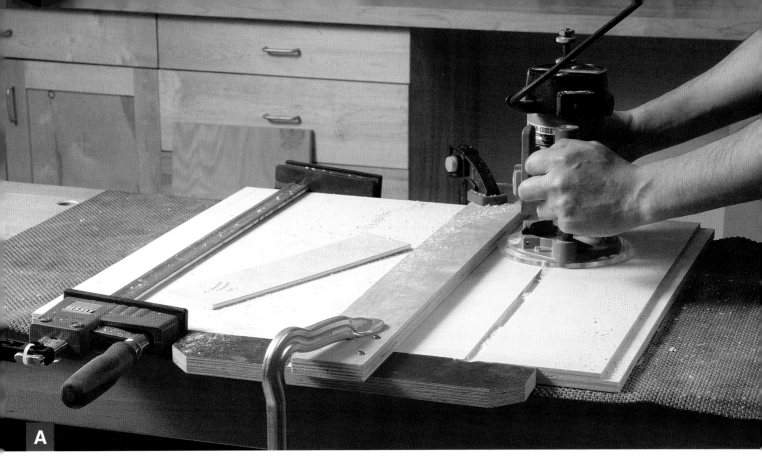

A

Set the crossbar against the edge, clamp the opposite end of the fence, and rout from left to right.

## Guides for Dadoes, Grooves, and Rabbets
T-squares, straightedges, and offset gauges.

T-squares and straightedges are used for cutting dadoes (**Photo A**), grooves, and rabbets, trimming sheet goods, and straightening edges. Routing might be a tad slower than using a tablesaw, but think savings: a $20 bit can cut just as cleanly as a $200 dado head.

Make the guide fence at least 6" longer than the piece you plan to rout. Fasten the fence to the crossbar with a single screw; then check the assembly with a reliable square (such as a 12" drafting triangle) before driving the remaining fasteners.

The first time you use your jig, you're likely to rout into the crossbar with your bit. This notch can help with positioning, but an offset gauge (**Photos B and C**) provides a more reliable means of positioning (especially after you've nipped the crossbar with a few different bits).

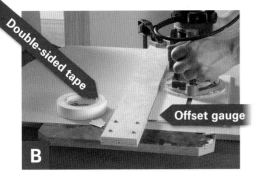

Double-sided tape

Offset gauge

B

To make an offset gauge, affix a piece of scrap against the fence and rout to width.

Offset gauge

C

Place the gauge against the fence to locate the bit's position. Clamp the T-square before routing.

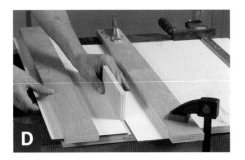

Built-in offset guides attached to the fence can save time when routing dadoes that are wider than the bit (**Photo D**). Attach ⅛"-thick Marlite or hardboard to the back face of the fence with double-sided tape, and then run the router along both fences to trim the material to exact width. (Note the router and bit used with the jigs so that you can reuse the same guides in the future.)

To position fences with built-in guides, simply set the stock between the two built-in offsets.

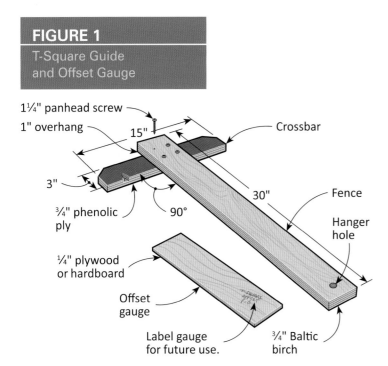

## FIGURE 1
### T-Square Guide and Offset Gauge

1¼" panhead screw
1" overhang
15"
Crossbar
3"
¾" phenolic ply
90°
30"
Fence
Hanger hole
¼" plywood or hardboard
Offset gauge
Label gauge for future use.
¾" Baltic birch

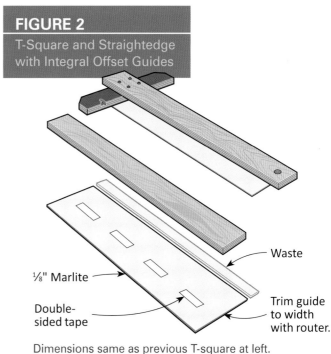

## FIGURE 2
### T-Square and Straightedge with Integral Offset Guides

Waste
⅛" Marlite
Double-sided tape
Trim guide to width with router.

Dimensions same as previous T-square at left.

A

Measure and drill a pivot hole wherever needed. Use the drill bit as your pivot point.

# Trammels for Circles and Arcs

## The Basic Trammel

To get a router to go in circles, all you need is a means of smoothly moving the router around a point. This basic trammel design is simple (**Photo A**), but it works and can be easily modified for larger diameters. (The brace isn't a necessity, but for jigs longer than 24" it provides extra rigidity.)

To use the jig, measure out from the bit and drill a hole in the base. Then drill a pivot hole in your workpiece. Using the bit as your pivot, mount the base to the workpiece. To make the cut, switch on the router and plunge down no more than ¼" deep, and then feed the router counterclockwise around the workpiece.

**FIGURE 1**

Basic Trammel

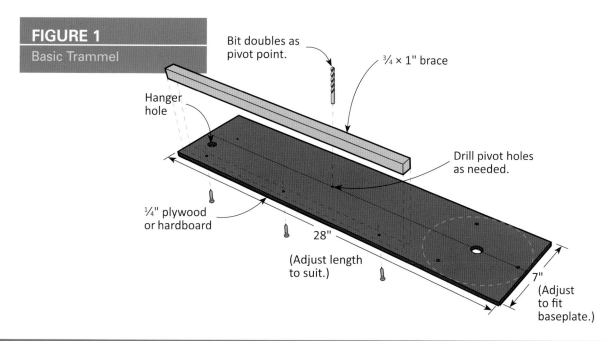

Bit doubles as pivot point.

¾ × 1" brace

Hanger hole

Drill pivot holes as needed.

¼" plywood or hardboard

28"

(Adjust length to suit.)

7"

(Adjust to fit baseplate.)

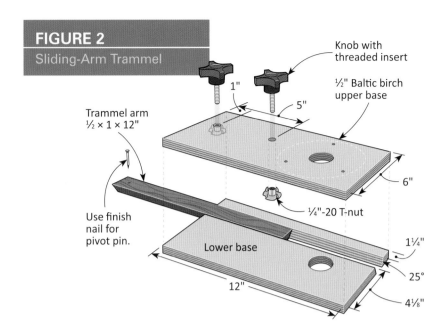

**FIGURE 2**
Sliding-Arm Trammel

Knob with threaded insert

½" Baltic birch upper base

1"

5"

Trammel arm
½ × 1 × 12"

6"

Use finish nail for pivot pin.

¼"-20 T-nut

Lower base

1¼"

25°

12"

4⅛"

## Sliding-Arm Trammel

This jig's adjustable trammel arm (**Photo B**) is easier to set than the basic trammel. With the pin end of the trammel arm inside the lower base, the jig can cut circles as small as 1½" in diameter; by reversing the arm, it can rout circles up to 22".

To make this jig, cut the base parts slightly oversize; then adjust your tablesaw blade to 25°, and rip the opposing edges of the bottom plywood parts and both edges of the trammel arm. Set the router on the upper base, rotate it to allow the sliding arm to fit between the baseplate screws, and then mark out the holes and insert the T-nuts. Sandwich the sliding arm between the lower base pieces, and then fasten the two pieces to the upper base, using glue or pin nails. If the lower base extends past the upper base, rip the edges flush.

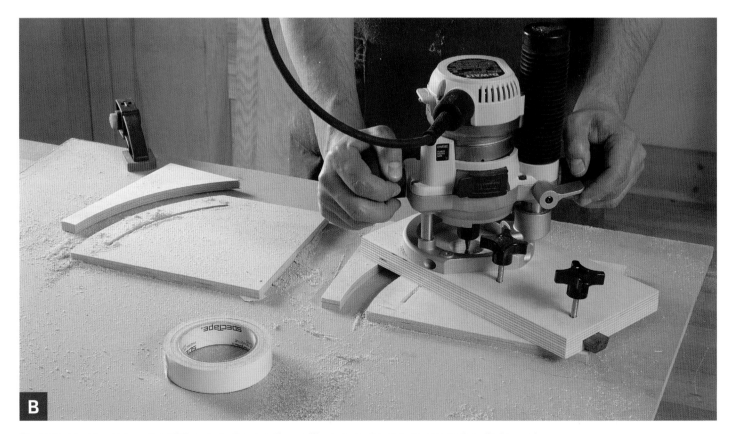

**B**

Threaded knobs secure the sliding arm. For smaller radii, reverse the arm to move the pin inward.

**A**

Move the router counterclockwise so that the bit's rotation pulls the guide to the workpiece edge.

## Guides for Edges and Face Work

### Pivot-Strip Edge Guide

Unlike a straightedge, an edge guide ensures that cuts are parallel to the ends or edges of a workpiece because it's guided by the work. This small-scale guide excels at cutting rabbets (**Photo A**), but you can also pivot the guide's fence to rout grooves up to about 4" away from the edge. (For larger cutting capacity, make a larger base.) Despite this jig's simplicity, it outperforms some of the flimsier commercial guides that tend to slip in use. This screwed-in strip isn't going to move.

With minor adjustments, you can also use the jig to rout a series of evenly spaced dadoes. Simply size the fence to fit the desired dado. Fasten the strip to one corner, and then adjust the arm to the desired position. After routing your first dado (either with this jig or a T-square guide), set the fence in the first dado and rout the next.

**FIGURE 1**
Pivot-Strip Edge Guide

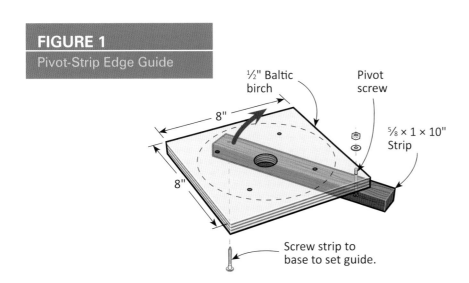

½" Baltic birch

Pivot screw

8"

8"

⅝ × 1 × 10" Strip

Screw strip to base to set guide.

**FIGURE 2**
Double-Fence Edge Guide

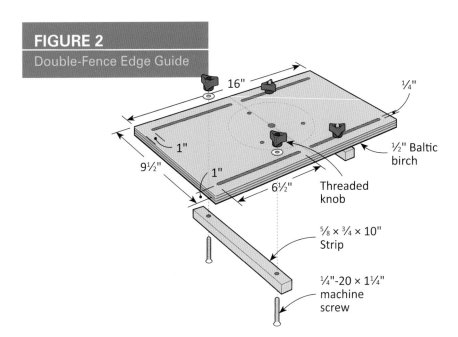

16"

¼"

1"

9½"

1"

6½"

½" Baltic birch

Threaded knob

⅝ × ¾ × 10" Strip

¼"-20 × 1¼" machine screw

## Double-Fence Edge Guide

Routers sometimes run off course, especially when used on narrow stock or along an edge. This guide prevents this by providing a pair of lockable fences. (This model can also be used with a single fence, for rabbets and dadoes.) Use your router table and a ¼"-diameter straight bit to make the slots in the base. Attach stops to the table's fence to control the start and end of the cut.

For routing flutes, like those shown in **Photo B**, lay out the center lines for each cove cut on a scrap piece of stock that's the same width as your workpiece. Align the center line on the jig with your layout lines, slide the fences so they rest against the edges of your workpiece, and make a test cut.

**B**

A pair of fences keeps the router on track. Marking the bit's location on the base makes the jig easier to set.

When using a fixed based router, brace the base against a cleat and tip the bit into the work.

## Mortising Guides

### Base-Guided Template

This mortising jig only requires a router and straight or spiral bit. And because the cutout is the exact size of the desired mortise, you can check the layout against the mortise before routing your workpiece.

To make this jig, lay out the mortise on a scrap of hardboard large enough to support the router and cleats. Then use an offset gauge (see page 41) to lay out the cleat locations. Now attach the cleats with double-faced tape. (By arranging the cleats as shown in **Photo A**, you won't need to waste time trimming them to exact length.)

Rout through the base and then double-check the size of the cutout. Finally, clamp or stick the template to your workpiece and rout.

### FIGURE 1
Base-Guided Template

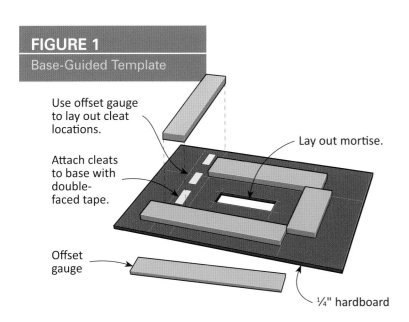

Use offset gauge to lay out cleat locations.

Attach cleats to base with double-faced tape.

Lay out mortise.

Offset gauge

¼" hardboard

## FIGURE 2
### Mortising Platform

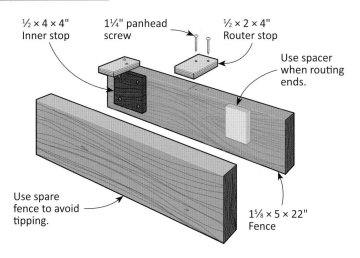

½ × 4 × 4"
Inner stop

1¼" panhead
screw

½ × 2 × 4"
Router stop

Use spacer
when routing
ends.

Use spare
fence to avoid
tipping.

1⅝ × 5 × 22"
Fence

## Mortising Platform

A wide variety of loose-tenon mortising jigs exist, but this one (**Photo B**) boils things down to the basics. Thick fences support the router's base and provide a long reference edge. Stops control the length of cut and help register the workpiece flush with the fence's top edge. *(Note: Depending on the material you're routing, you may not need the second fence.)*

Build the jig as shown in **Figure 2**. To set up the jig, lay out your mortises on your workpiece, and then butt your stock to the inner stop and clamp it to the fence. Position your router on the fence, and then adjust your edge guide so that the bit's centered between your layout lines. Attach the router stops so that the bit can't cut past your mortise lines.

To rout the mortise, first plunge the bit to full depth on each end. Then working in ¼" increments, rout out the waste between the two holes. To feed the router so that the bit's rotation pulls the guide to the work, position the fence as shown in **Photo C** and make your cutting passes from right to left.

Set the workpiece against the inner stop. Then attach the router stops to adjust the length of the mortise.

Register the edge of the workpiece against the inner stop when routing ends.

# CHAPTER 3
# HELP FOR OTHER TOOLS

## Tricked-Out Drill-Press Table
Can boring get interesting? With this design it just did.

After studying a variety of woodworking drill-press tables going back the last two decades, and having made a couple along the way, I took up the challenge of designing what I feel is the most versatile and functional fixture for the home shop. I wanted it to incorporate the latest quality hardware and materials while keeping the cost reasonable. I employed a selection of knobs, Kreg Mini T-Trak, screws, hold-downs, and hard-wearing phenolic-faced plywood, an ideal product for shop use.

Beyond materials, I wanted the fixture do it all. I spec'd the table to include replaceable hardboard inserts, hold-downs, sturdy extensions tables that expand the width to a whopping 46¾", and adjustable fence systems, complete with stops. I also added a sliding and locking vertical table for boring into the ends of workpieces that you can quickly remove when not in use. Finally, by attaching the horizontal table to a box structure, I created three handy compartments for storing bits and accessories. The assembly installs easily on a standard sized table.

OVERALL DIMENSIONS | 46¾"w × 15"d × 6⅛"h
(EXTENSION TABLES OPEN; CLOSED, 29¾"w)

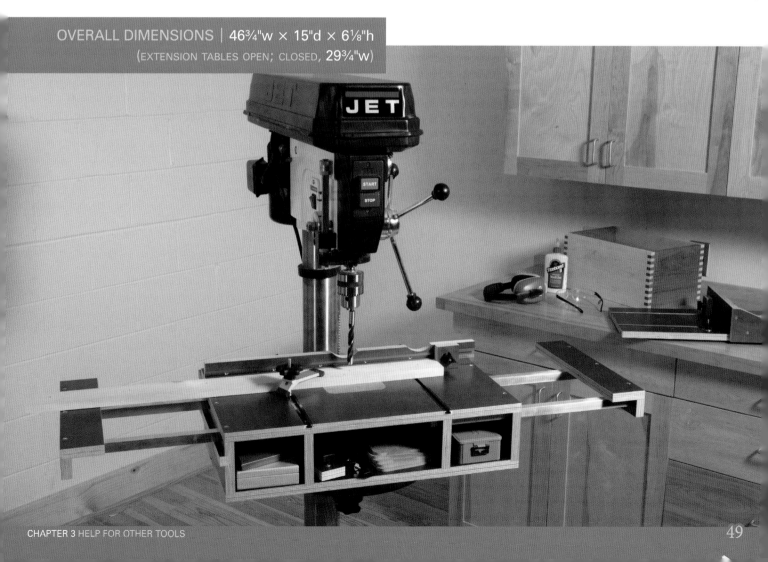

## FIGURE 1

Drill-Press Table
Exploded View

**NOTE:** For the items needed to make the table, see the **Convenience-Plus Buying Guide** on page 54. Also, refer to the handy **Cut List**, page 54.

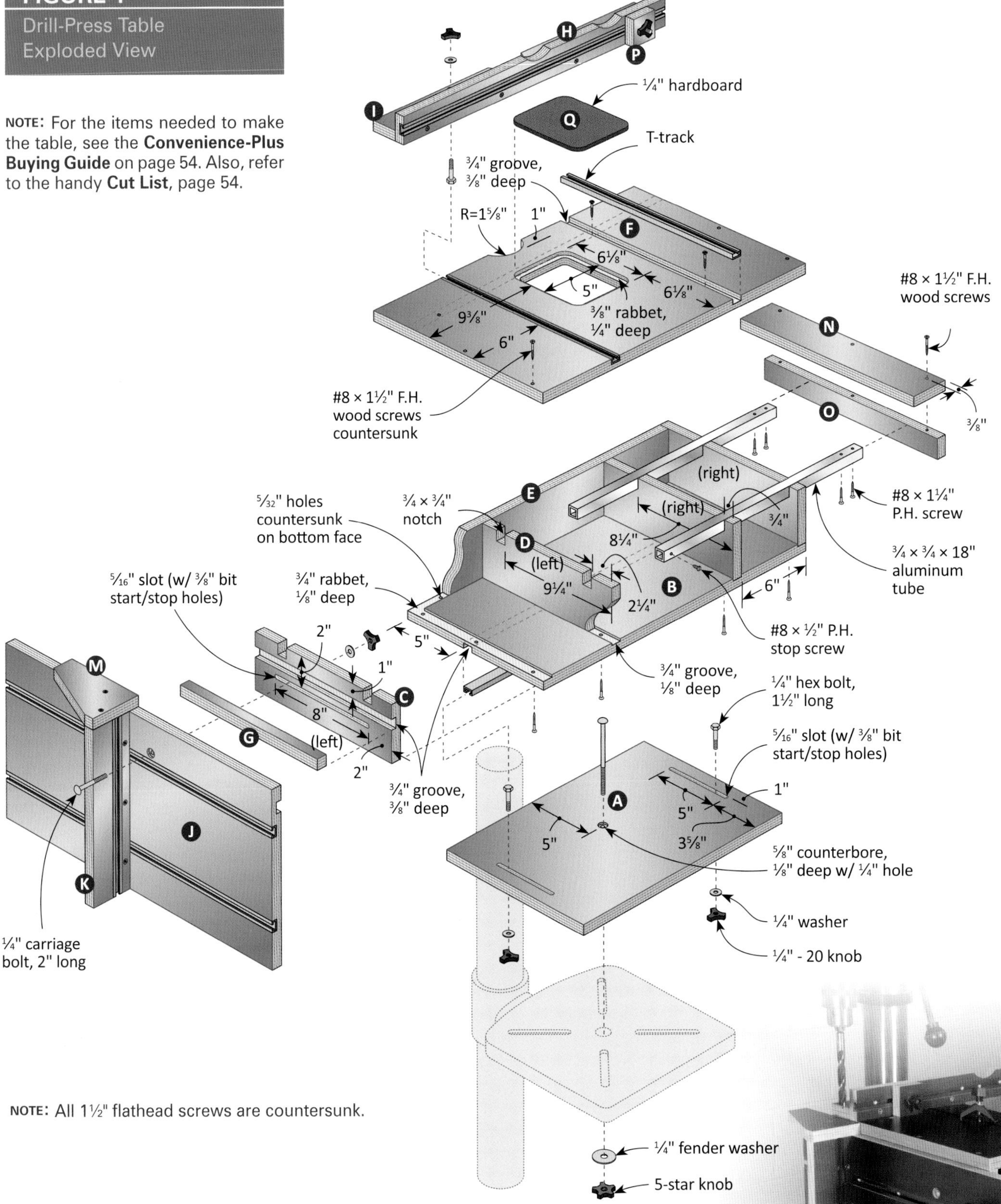

H
P
I
¼" hardboard
Q
T-track
¾" groove, ⅜" deep
R=1⅝"
1"
F
6⅛"
5"
6⅛"
9⅜"
⅜" rabbet, ¼" deep
6"
#8 × 1½" F.H. wood screws
N
#8 × 1½" F.H. wood screws countersunk
O
⅜"
(right)
E
5⁄32" holes countersunk on bottom face
¾ × ¾" notch
(right)
¾"
#8 × 1¼" P.H. screw
8¼"
D
(left)
¾ × ¾ × 18" aluminum tube
9¼"
B
6"
5⁄16" slot (w/ ⅜" bit start/stop holes)
¾" rabbet, ⅛" deep
2¼"
2"
5"
#8 × ½" P.H. stop screw
M
1"
C
¾" groove, ⅛" deep
8"
¼" hex bolt, 1½" long
G
(left)
2"
5⁄16" slot (w/ ⅜" bit start/stop holes)
¾" groove, ⅜" deep
J
A
1"
5"
5"
3⅝"
⅝" counterbore, ⅛" deep w/ ¼" hole
K
¼" washer
¼" carriage bolt, 2" long
¼" - 20 knob
¼" fender washer
5-star knob


**NOTE:** All 1½" flathead screws are countersunk.

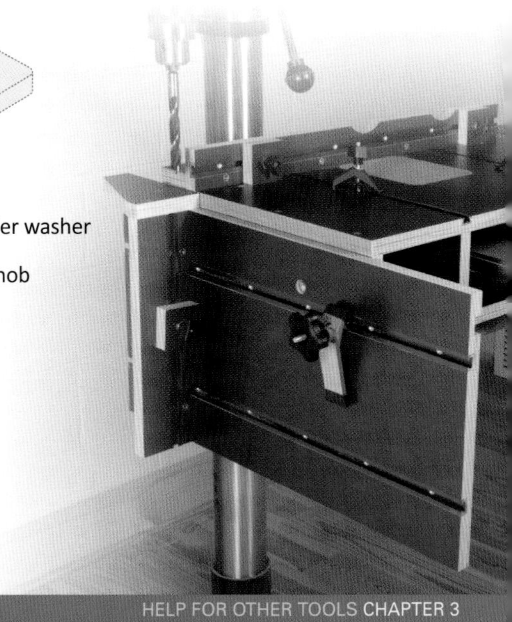

**Stop hole**

**Start hole**

**A**

With the bit in the start hole and the fence and stops in place, move the workpiece as shown to cut the slot.

**Miter gauge extension**

**B**

Team up a miter gauge extension with the saw's fence to cut the notches for the aluminum tubes.

## Make the platform and box

**1** Cut the platform (A), box bottom (B), sides (C), dividers (D), back (E), and horizontal table (F) to the sizes listed in the **Cut List**.

**2** To secure the platform (A) to your drill-press table, drill the ⅝" counterbored recess ⅛" deep with a ¼" through-hole where shown in **Figure 1**.

### TIP ALERT

When plunge-cutting on the tablesaw, prevent the cutout from moving and contacting the blade after the final cut by securing it with tape.

**3** Lay out the slots on platform (A) and the left side (C) where shown. Now, at your drill press and using a clamped-on fence, drill the ⅜" bit start and stop holes at both ends of the slot. Move to your router table, and chuck in a ⁵⁄₁₆" straight bit. Use the holes in the platform (and later the side) to set up the fence and infeed and outfeed stops by lowering and centering the holes in the parts over the bit and adjusting the fence and stops accordingly. Next, rout the slots, as shown in **Photo A**.

**4** Equip your tablesaw with a ¾" dado set, and raise it to cut ⅜" deep. Note the locations of the grooves for the T-track in the box bottom (B), left side (C), and horizontal table (F). Adjust your fence as needed, and cut the grooves in these parts.

**5** Lower the dado set to ⅛", adjust the fence, and cut the grooves on the top face of the box bottom (B) for the dividers (D) where shown in **Figure 1**. Add a sacrificial fence to the saw's fence, adjust the fence, and cut the rabbets in the bottom for receiving the sides (C) and back (E).

**6** Cut the ¾ × ¾" notches with your dado blade in the sides (C) and dividers (D) for the extension tubes. (Note: To enable the extension arms to retract into the base, the notches on the left side are offset from those on the right. Measuring from the front edges, lay out and label each part. Indicate the front edges as well, to avoid confusion.) Add a miter gauge extension fence, adjust the saw fence to serve as a stop, and carefully cut the notches as shown in **Photo B**. Check the notches with a tube to ensure a proper sliding fit.

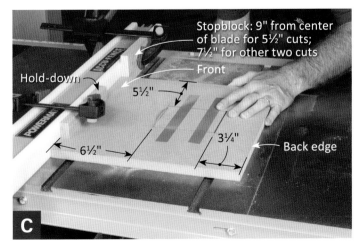

**Stopblock: 9" from center of blade for 5½" cuts; 7½" for other two cuts**

**Front**

**Hold-down**

5½"

6½"

3¼"

**Back edge**

**C**

With the workpiece pressed firmly to the table with a hold-down and hand, raise the blade through it to complete the cutout in the jig.

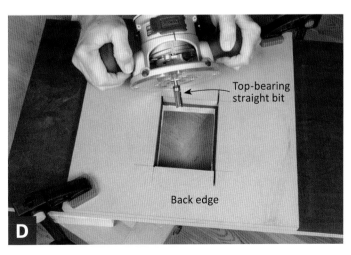

**Top-bearing straight bit**

**Back edge**

**D**

Run the pattern cutting bit clockwise around the template to rout a cutout with clean, square edges.

**7** Cut the glide strip (G) to size. Then glue and clamp it in the groove in the left side (C).

**8** To create the opening in the horizontal table (F) for the replaceable inserts (Q), make a simple one-time-use template with a rectangular opening having square corners and straight edges. Cut a ¾" piece of MDF to 15" square. Label one edge "front" and the opposing edge "back." Next, lay out the opening, using the distances from the edges of the workpiece to the saw blade in **Photo C**. To make the first of two side cuts, set up a stopblock 9" back from the center of the blade. Adjust the fence 5½" from the blade; lower the blade. Place the workpiece against the fence and stop, securing it at one edge with a clamped hold-down block. Turn on the saw and raise the blade through the workpiece until it intersects the perpendicular layout lines. Lower the blade, flip the workpiece edge for edge, and similarly cut the opposing side kerf. Flip the piece again, layout face up. Now using the dimensions in the photo, adjust the stop and fence and make the remaining cuts.

**9** Center the jig between the ends on the horizontal table (F) and clamp it in place. Then mark the opening to be cut out and remove the template. Drill a start hole, and then jigsaw the opening, cutting ⅛" inside the marked line. Now reposition the jig over the hole and clamp it to the table. With a router and ½" pattern cutting bit, rout the opening (**Photo D**).

**10** Chuck a ⅜" rabbeting bit in your handheld router, and set the cut depth to the thickness of the replaceable inserts (Q). Rout around the opening.

**11** Lay out and bandsaw the radius notch for the drill-press post on the back edge of horizontal table (F) where shown in **Figure 1**.

## FIGURE 2
### Fence and Stop

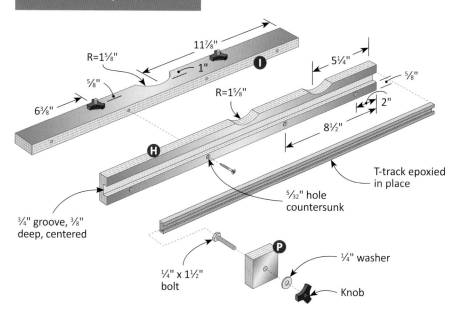

## FIGURE 3
### Vertical Sliding Table

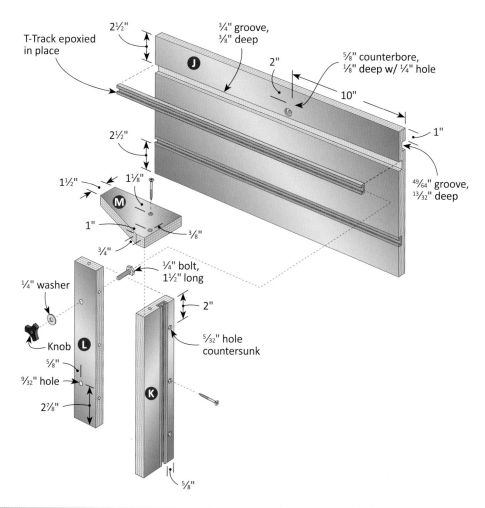

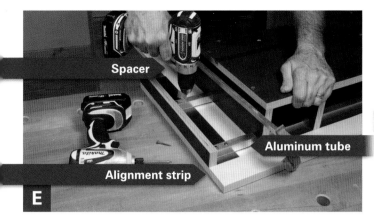

Spacer

Aluminum tube

Alignment strip

**E**

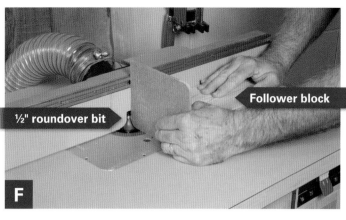

½" roundover bit

Follower block

**F**

With the extension assembly aligned with the box, drill the holes for securing the aluminum tubes with screws.

Using a 2-by follower block for safety and support, rout the ½" corner radii on a batch of replaceable inserts.

**12** Lay out and drill the countersunk shank holes where shown for the box bottom (B) and horizontal table (F).

**13** Clamp the box bottom (B), sides (C), dividers (D), back (E), and the horizontal table (F) together, referring to **Figure 1**. Then drill the pilot holes into the mating parts using the shank holes as guides. Drive the screws to complete the box assembly.

**TIP ALERT**

To keep the extension tables from accidently pulling out completely when in use, add stop screws to the interior ends of the aluminum tubes.

**Build the fences and extension tables**

**1** Cut the horizontal fence face (H), horizontal fence support (I), vertical table (J), vertical fence face (K), vertical fence support (L), vertical fence end (M), extension tabletop (N), extension table side (O), and stops (P) to the sizes listed in the **Cut List**.

**2** Lay out and cut all the dadoes and grooves for the T-track in the horizontal fence face (H) vertical fence face (K), and vertical table (J). See **Figures 2** and **3**. Lay out and cut the groove on the inside face of the vertical table for the glide strip (G). Widen the groove to $^{49}/_{64}$" and cut it to a depth of $^{13}/_{32}$" to allow for sliding action.

**3** Layout the radii for the curved notches for the drill-press chuck and handle in the horizontal fence face (H) and for the drill-press post in the horizontal fence support (I), where shown in **Figure 2**. Bandsaw the notches and drum-sand them smooth.

**4** Drill the assembly holes for the fences (H, I and K, L, M) and extension tables (N, O), where shown in **Figures 1, 2,** and **3**. Also drill the holes for the hex head and carriage bolts, including the centered holes in stops (P). Note that the carriage bolt hole in the vertical table (J) is counterbored. Now clamp and screw the mating parts together.

**5** Set up your tablesaw with an 80-tooth carbide blade, zero-clearance insert, and miter gauge with an extension fence to back up the part. Now cut the T-track pieces to size. Clean the T-tracks to remove any oil that might interfere with making a good bond. Spread epoxy in the T-track grooves with glue brushes, and fit and clamp the tracks in place, wiping up any squeeze-out with rubbing alcohol. Let cure.

**6** Cut the aluminum tubes to 18" long, and drill a pair of attachment holes on the ends of each tube (**Figure 1**). Now, turn the box assembly over, horizontal table face-down. Insert the tubes into the notches and fit one extension table assembly (N, O) into position alongside the box assembly. Cut and fit a 3" spacer between the two tables to allow room for a cordless drill. Then clamp a pair of straightedge strips at the front and back of the assembly to align the tables. Mark pilot holes on the underside of the extension table, guiding on the tube holes. Drill the pilot holes in the table (**Photo E**), then drive the screws, securing the tubes. Repeat for the other extension table. Flip the box assembly table side up.

**7** From ¼" hardboard, cut a batch of replaceable inserts (Q) to size. Radius the corners with a ½" round-over bit in a router table as shown in **Photo F,** or stack-bandsaw and disc-sand several pieces using the same ½" radius.

## Final assembly

**1** Insert a ¼ × 6" carriage bolt through the platform (A), and then the center of the drill-press table, securing it with a fender washer and five-star knob.

**2** Next, insert the ¼ × 1½" hex bolts into the slots in platform (A), and loosely hold them in place with washers and three-star knobs. Fit the bolt heads into the T-track at the bottom of the box assembly. Center the assembly (and insert opening) under the chuck. Tighten the knobs.

**3** To attach the vertical table (J) to the box assembly, first remove the left-hand extension table. Fit the table's groove onto the glide strip (G), and secure the table with a 2" carriage bolt, fender washer, and knob. Change out the assemblies as needed.

**4** Attach the fences to both tables with the hex head bolts, washers, and three-star knobs. Similarly add the stops (P). Finally, drop a replaceable insert in the rabbeted opening, and you're ready for business.

## Convenience-Plus Buying Guide

| | | |
|---|---|---|
| ☐ | 1 | Phenolic-Faced MultiPly (plywood), ¾ × 24 × 48", qty. 2 |
| ☐ | 2 | Kreg Mini Trak, ¼" T-track, qty. 3 |
| ☐ | 3 | Woodpeckers Deluxe Hold-Down Clamp |
| ☐ | 4 | Kreg Trak Clamp, qty. 2 |
| ☐ | 5 | Incra Build-it System, ¼" - 20 Knob Kit, qty. 2 |
| ☐ | 6 | 5-Star Knob w/Through-Hole ¼" – 20 insert |
| ☐ | 7 | Flathead Screws, Extra Torque, Square Drive, #8 × 1½", qty. 100 |
| ☐ | 8 | System Three 5-Minute Epoxy, ½ pt. |
| ☐ | 9 | Disposable Glue Brushes, ½" width, qty. 48 |

## Drill-Press Table Cut List

| | PART | THICKNESS | WIDTH | LENGTH | QTY. | MAT'L |
|---|---|---|---|---|---|---|
| A | Platform | ¾" | 12" | 18" | 1 | PP |
| B | Box bottom | ¾" | 12" | 23¾" | 1 | PP |
| C | Sides | ¾" | 4" | 12" | 1 | PP |
| D | Dividers | ¾" | 4" | 11¼" | 2 | PP |
| E | Back | ¾" | 4" | 22¼" | 1 | PP |
| F | Horizontal table | ¾" | 15" | 23¾" | 1 | PP |
| G | Glide strip | ¾" | ¾" | 12" | 1 | PP |
| H | Horizontal fence face | ¾" | 2" | 23¾" | 1 | PP |
| I | Horizontal fence support | ¾" | 3" | 23¾" | 1 | PP |
| J | Vertical table | ¾" | 12" | 23¾" | 1 | PP |
| K | Vertical fence face | ¾" | 3" | 12" | 1 | PP |
| L | Vertical fence support | ¾" | 2" | 12" | 1 | PP |
| M | Vertical fence end | ¾" | 3¾" | 6" | 1 | PP |
| N | Extension tabletop | ¾" | 3" | 15" | 2 | PP |
| O | Extension table side | ¾" | 1½" | 15" | 2 | PP |
| P | Stops | ¾" | 2" | 2" | 3 | PP |
| Q | Replaceable inserts | ¼" | 5" | 6⅛" | As needed | H |

**Materials:** PP=Phenolic Plywood, H=Hardboard
**Hardware/Supplies:** (2) ¼" fender washers; (8) #8 ×1¼" panhead screws; (2) #8 × ½" panhead screws; (1) ¼ × 6" carriage bolt (measure for exact length); (1) ¼ × 2" carriage bolt; (2) ¾ × ¾" (square) aluminum tube, 3'.

## Two-Handed Jointer Pushpad

For added pressure and stability when face-jointing long stock, make and take advantage of this two-handed jointer pushpad.

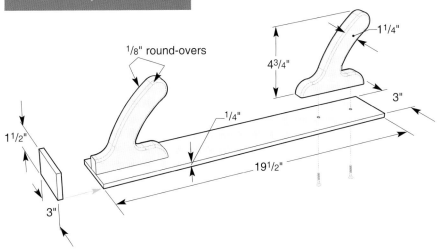

1/8" round-overs

1 1/4"

4 3/4"

3"

1 1/2"

1/4"

19 1/2"

3"

# Adjustable Planer Carrier Sled

This jig flattens the face of twisted boards, short ones included, and even those wider than your jointer's capacity. Place your stock on the board with the stop and then index the holes in the top component onto the dowels. Use pairs of tapered shims to immobilize the workpiece and remove any rocking motion.

## FIGURE 1
Adjustable Planer Carrier Sled

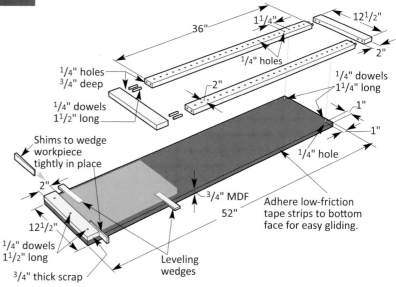

36"

$1^1/4$"

$12^1/2$"

$1/4$" holes

2"

$1/4$" holes
$3/4$" deep

$1/4$" dowels
$1^1/4$" long

$1/4$" dowels
$1^1/2$" long

2"

1"

1"

$1/4$" hole

Shims to wedge workpiece tightly in place

2"

$3/4$" MDF

52"

Adhere low-friction tape strips to bottom face for easy gliding.

$12^1/2$"

$1/4$" dowels
$1^1/2$" long

Leveling wedges

$3/4$" thick scrap

# Bandsaw Resaw Jig
### Slice even slabs from thicker stock.

This resaw jig reduces waste and improves the quality of the cut pieces. At right, the craftsman inserts a walnut board between the jig and the fence. Two featherboards mounted on short pieces of angle iron allow them to be positioned both vertically and horizontally, depending on the height and thickness of the board. A tight, secure fit ensures resawn boards will have uniform thickness and smoothness. The jig itself is clamped to the bandsaw table.

## FIGURE 1
Bandsaw Resaw Jig

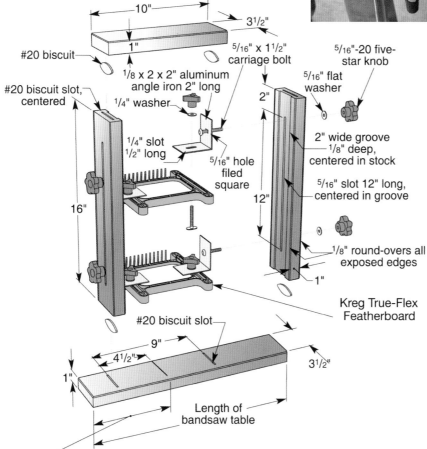

10"

3 1/2"

1"

#20 biscuit

5/16" x 1 1/2" carriage bolt

5/16"-20 five-star knob

#20 biscuit slot, centered

1/8 x 2 x 2" aluminum angle iron 2" long

1/4" washer

5/16" flat washer

2"

2" wide groove 1/8" deep, centered in stock

1/4" slot 1/2" long

5/16" hole filed square

5/16" slot 12" long, centered in groove

16"

12"

1/8" round-overs all exposed edges

1"

Kreg True-Flex Featherboard

#20 biscuit slot

9"

4 1/2"

1"

3 1/2"

Length of bandsaw table

Distance from front of bandsaw table to front of blade must be centered between uprights.

## Circle-Sanding Jig
Sand round edges to perfection.

This disc sander circle-sanding jig is easily constructed from plywood. By adjusting the knob, you can change the diameter of the circle you are sanding. Use it, for example, for sanding circular parts in wooden toys and puzzles.

### FIGURE 1
Circle-Sanding Jig

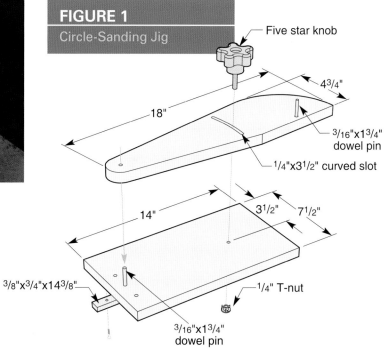

Five star knob

4³/₄"

18"

³/₁₆"x1³/₄" dowel pin

¹/₄"x3¹/₂" curved slot

14"

3¹/₂"    7¹/₂"

³/₈"x³/₄"x14³/₈"

¹/₄" T-nut

³/₁₆"x1³/₄" dowel pin

# Woodturner's Bowl Press

This press is designed to glue up segmented and staved turnings. The frame and base are made of solid stock and a piece of Baltic birch plywood. Pressure is applied by a 1" dowel handle fitted into a German 1¼ x 18" bench screw. The screw's foot pad, which was made at a machinist's shop, attaches with an Allen screw.

**FIGURE 1**
Woodturner's Bowl Press

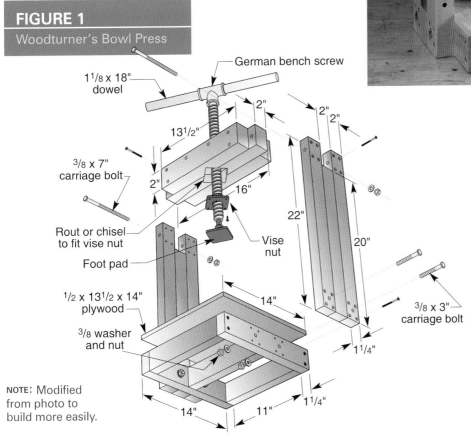

German bench screw

1¹/8 x 18" dowel

³/8 x 7" carriage bolt

13¹/2"

2"

2"

2"

2"

16"

22"

20"

Rout or chisel to fit vise nut

Foot pad

Vise nut

1/2 x 13¹/2 x 14" plywood

³/8 washer and nut

14"

1¹/4"

³/8 x 3" carriage bolt

14"

11"

1¹/4"

1¹/4"

NOTE: Modified from photo to build more easily.

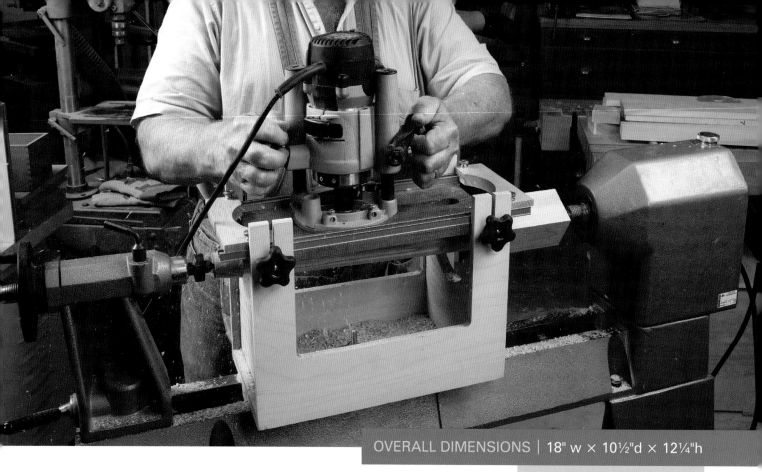

## Spindle-Fluting Lathe Jig

### Get repeatable results every time.

**M**aking identical flutes of the same length and depth and spaced evenly around the circumference of a tapered or cylindrical spindle such as a table leg requires a lathe, router—and one more thing—a precision jig. Mounted to your lathe, this accommodating shop project features a router platform that adjusts parallel to the workpiece surface for flutes of a consistent depth from one end to the other. Attached to the platform are T-track runners that support sliding stops. These lock in place, letting you create flutes of a repeatable desired length. Another locking mechanism secures the jig's base to the lathe's ways. Here's how to build the jig and put it to work.

### NOTE

Made from scrap plywood, hardwood, and store-bought hardware, this jig allows you to rout flutes up to 10" long. To cut longer flutes and to customize the jig to your lathe, follow the instructions and use the **Cut List** dimensions only as a general reference.

### Build the jig

**1** Cut the jig bottom (A) from ¾" hardwood plywood to the width in the **Cut List** on page 63 and to the desired length. The listed width allows you to rout flutes in cylinders up to 5" in diameter. Add 1" of bottom length for each additional 1" of desired flute length. After cutting the bottom to size, drill the centered ⅜" hole (**Figure 1**).

**2** From ½" plywood, cut the sides (B) to size. For the width, measure the distance from the ways to the center of the spindle, and add 4" to 6". For the side lengths, 15" works well for 10"-long or shorter flutes. Add 1" for each additional 1" of flute length.

## FIGURE 1

Spindle-Fluting Lathe Jig Exploded View

**NOTE:** For the items needed to make the jig, see the **Convenience-Plus Buying Guide** on page 63. Also, refer to the handy **Cut List** (page 63).

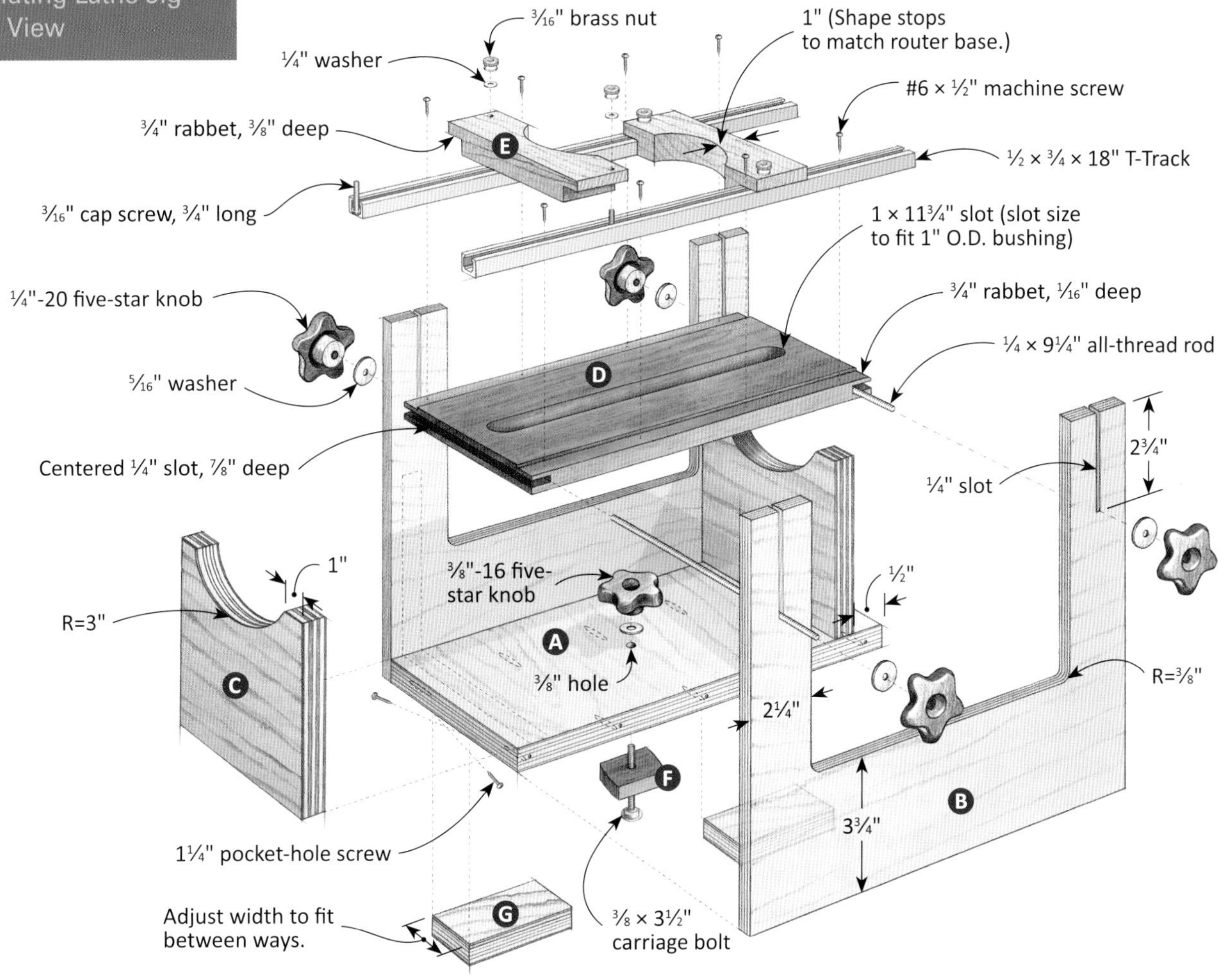

3/16" brass nut
1" (Shape stops to match router base.)
1/4" washer
#6 × 1/2" machine screw
3/4" rabbet, 3/8" deep
E
1/2 × 3/4 × 18" T-Track
3/16" cap screw, 3/4" long
1 × 11 3/4" slot (slot size to fit 1" O.D. bushing)
1/4"-20 five-star knob
3/4" rabbet, 1/16" deep
1/4 × 9 1/4" all-thread rod
5/16" washer
D
Centered 1/4" slot, 7/8" deep
2 3/4"
1/4" slot
1"
R=3"
3/8"-16 five-star knob
1/2"
A
3/8" hole
C
R=3/8"
2 1/4"
F
B
3 3/4"
1 1/4" pocket-hole screw
Adjust width to fit between ways.
G
3/8 × 3 1/2" carriage bolt


**3** Lay out and cut the windows in the sides (B), as shown in **Figure 1**, using a bandsaw or jigsaw. Saw just outside the line, and then sand the rough edges smooth.

**4** Mark the centered ¼" wide by 2¾" deep slots in the sides (B) (**Figure 1**), and cut these to length at the router table, using a straight bit, router fence, and stop. To do this, raise the bit ¼", and set the stop on the outfeed side of the fence. Make the initial cut for one slot, and then flip the piece end for end to cut the other slot. Similarly, rout the other side part. Raise the bit, and repeat the procedure as needed to rout slots in both sides.

**5** Cut the ends (C) from ¾" plywood to the same side-to-side width as the bottom (A). Determine the width by measuring the distance from the lathe ways to the center of the spindle and subtracting 2½". Lay out the curves along the inside edges to match your router base and bandsaw them to shape (**Figure 1**).

**6** Drill pocket holes in the bottom (A), as shown in **Figure 1**, and then drive pocket-hole screws to attach the bottom to the sides (B). (Or simply drive screws through the sides and into the base.) Fit and glue the ends (C) in place.

**7** Plane a piece of hardwood to ⅝" thick for the adjustable platform (D). Rip it to a width that measures the same as the distance between the sides (B), less 1/16". (This allows for easy adjustment between the sides.) Now, crosscut the piece to 1" less than the length of the sides (B).

**8** Lay out the centered 1"-wide slot (sized for a 1" OD router guide bushing) on the adjustable platform (D). Make the slot's length at least 1" longer than the length of your intended flutes. Next, using a 1" Forstner bit in a drill press, bore centered holes inside the ends of the laid out slot. Saw out the waste between the holes, staying inside the lines.

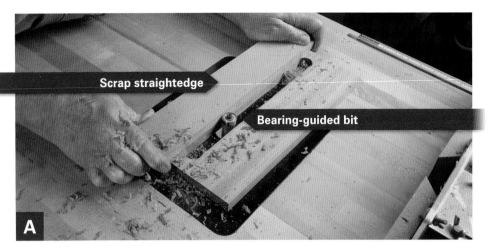

**Scrap straightedge**

**Bearing-guided bit**

**A**

Trim off the waste in the slot by guiding off the scrapwood straightedge.

**B**

Cut a centered slot in both ends of the adjustable platform with an auxiliary tall fence and pushstick.

**9** Using double-faced tape, adhere a straight piece of scrap onto the top face of the adjustable platform (D), tangent with the holes drilled in **Step 8**. Chuck a bottom-bearing flush-trim bit in your table-mounted router, and then trim off the remaining waste in the slot, as shown in **Photo A**. Achieving a slot with perfectly parallel edges is critical to the jig's fluting accuracy.

**10** Raise the tablesaw blade to ⅞", and add an auxiliary tall fence to the saw's fence with double-faced tape. Now, with a pushstick, cut a centered slot in the ends of the adjustable platform (D), as shown in **Photo B**. Adjust the fence as needed to cut a centered ¼" slot, flipping the workpiece edge for edge and end for end with each fence adjustment. Test-fit the all-thread rod (see **Figure 1**) in the slots.

**11** With a tablesaw or a straight bit in a table-mounted router, cut the ¾" rabbets ¹⁄₁₆" deep in the top face of the adjustable platform (D). Cut two T-tracks 4" longer than the length of the platform, and install them centered in the rabbets with screws.

**12** Rip a 2"-wide piece of ¾" hardwood. From it, crosscut two stops (E) that are equal in length to the width of the adjustable platform (D). Next, rabbet the ends (**Figure 1**), and mark the inside edge of each piece. Drill ¼" holes in the rabbets ⅜" from the ends and ½" from the inside edges. Finally, as a way to maximize the travel distance for the router without further extending the T-tracks, I cut out arcs on the inside edges of the stops, but straight-edged stops would work equally well. Add the washers and five-star knobs to the end of the all-thread rod.

### Fit the jig to your lathe

**1** Measure the distance between the inside walls beneath your lathe's ways. Then trim a ½"-thick to a width just under your ways' slot width from hardwood scrap. Cut the piece to ¾" longer than the distance between the ways' walls. Drill a ⅜" centered hole through the piece, and disc-sand a gentle arc on the ends, removing ⅜" from two opposing corners (**Figure 1**). You want this cam-action lock block (F) to jam between the ways' walls when tightened in place.

**TIP ALERT**

When turning parts to flute, make an extra sacrificial part or two to fine-tune your settings and get a handle on how the jig operates.

**2** Using the distance between the ways for the width of the ways spacers (G), cut two ¾"-thick pieces of plywood or hardwood to 3½" long. Test their fit between the ways and then center, glue, and pin them onto the jig's bottom (A).

**3** Insert the carriage bolt through the lock block (F), and add the washer and five-star knob. Test-fit the jig onto your lathe and tighten the knob.

### Put the jig to work

**1** Center the jig on the lathe bed between the headstock and tailstock, and lock it in place. Loosen the all-thread rod and hardware and lift off the adjustable platform (D). Secure your tapered or cylindrical turned workpiece between the centers.

**2** Mark the length and location of your flutes on the turning. Determine the number of flutes and set the detent on your headstock. You will need to be familiar with the number of detents on your particular lathe to know how to figure the degree of rotation and number of detents from one flute to the next. (The lathe I used had 24 evenly spaced detents over 360° of circumference. That meant that the distance between detents equaled 15° [360° ÷ 24 = 15°]. For the turned leg on page 60, which called for six flutes, I divided six into 360°. The resulting 60° was the spacing between each flute.

Fit a thin spacer between the platform and turning to establish the angle of the platform for a consistent flute depth from end to end.

Use the measurement between the edge of your router's baseplate and bit to set up the stops, guiding off the marks on your workpiece for the ends of the flute.

So I rotated the turning to every fourth detent [4 × 15° = 60°] to achieve the needed number of flutes.) Now, rotate the turning and stop where needed (based on your number of flutes). Note that the number of flutes must divide into the number of detents available and result in a whole number (24 ÷ 6 = 4) for you to use the jig. Make a pencil mark on the workpiece at each stop for easy, quick reference.

**3** Replace the platform (D). Slide a thin spacer such as ⅛" Baltic birch plywood between it and the turning, as shown in **Photo C**. Now lock the platform angle in place, and remove the spacer.

**4** Outfit your plunge-router baseplate with a 1" OD guide bushing, and chuck in the desired fluting or core-box bit. Mark the start and stop points of one flute on the workpiece. Next, measure the distance from the perimeter of the bit to the outside edge of the baseplate. Use this measurement and the start and stop marks to set up your stops (**Photo D**).

**5** Set the router on the platform (D), fitting the bushing in the slot. Lower the bit onto the turning. Guiding off of this bit depth, set up the plunge stops in increments to make multiple light cuts to the desired flute depth. Turn on the router and cut a shallow flute. Adjust the stop, and cut a deeper flute. Continue until you reach the needed depth. Rotate the piece, and cut the remaining flutes.

## Convenience-Plus Buying Guide

| | | |
|---|---|---|
| ☐ 1 | Five-Star Knob, ¼"-20, qty. 4 |
| ☐ 2 | Five-Star Knob, ⅜"-16 |
| ☐ 3 | Incra T-Track, ½ × ¾ × 36" |
| ☐ 4 | Kreg #8 × 1¼" Pocket-Hole Screws, 100/pkg. |

# Spindle-Fluting Jig Cut List

| | PART | THICKNESS | WIDTH | LENGTH | QTY. | MAT'L |
|---|---|---|---|---|---|---|
| A* | Bottom | ¾" | 13½" | 7¼" | 1 | Ply |
| B* | Sides | ½" | 11½" | 15" | 2 | Ply |
| C* | Ends | ¾" | 5¾" | 7¼" | 2 | Ply |
| D* | Adjustable platform | ¾" | 7³⁄₁₆" | 14" | 1 | HW |
| E* | Stops | ¾" | 2" | 7⅜" | 2 | HW |
| F* | Lock block | ½" | 1¾" | 2½" | 1 | HW |
| G* | Ways spacers | ¾" | 2" | 3½" | 2 | Ply |

**Materials:** Ply=Plywood, HW=Hardwood
**Hardware/Supplies:** (4) ³⁄₁₆" brass nuts; (4) ³⁄₁₆" cap screws, ¾" long; (1) ⅜" carriage bolt, 3 ½" long; (4) ¼" washers; (4) ⁵⁄₁₆" washers; (1) ⅜ " washer; (8) #6 × ½" machine screws; (1) ¼" all-thread rod, 11¼" long
\* Adjust the part dimensions to agree with your lathe and desired flute length. See instructions.

## Magnetic Hand-Plane Jointer Fence
### True a board's edges quickly.

Use rare-earth magnets and a rabbeted piece of maple to make a simple fence for your plane. The photo shows a Lie-Nielsen #62 plane. A shaped piece of wood glued at the front end of the fence helps house the plane while conforming to its shape. Recessed metal cups screwed in the fence hold the magnets that secure the iron plane in place. You'll find that the fence makes it infinitely easier to true a board's edges.

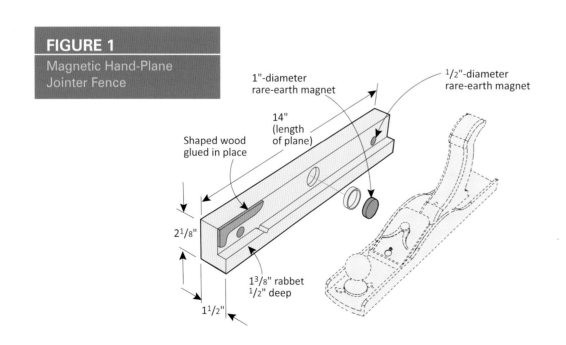

**FIGURE 1**

Magnetic Hand-Plane
Jointer Fence

1"-diameter
rare-earth magnet

$1/2$"-diameter
rare-earth magnet

14"
(length
of plane)

Shaped wood
glued in place

$2^1/8$"

$1^3/8$" rabbet
$1/2$" deep

$1^1/2$"

## Circular Saw Plywood Guide
### Cut straight edges fast.

Cutting large plywood panels down to size on a table saw can be a bit cumbersome, so this plywood cutting jig will serve you well. When down, the flip-up fence shows the exact location of your circular saw blade, eliminating a measuring step. Just measure one time, flip the board and cut the line with your saw. The jig is adaptable to other portable power tools, such as a router and jigsaw.

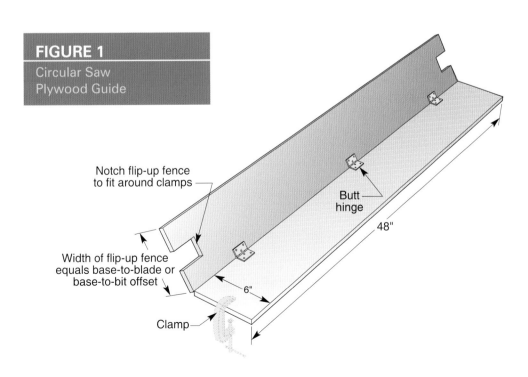

**FIGURE 1**
Circular Saw
Plywood Guide

Notch flip-up fence
to fit around clamps

Butt
hinge

48"

Width of flip-up fence
equals base-to-blade or
base-to-bit offset

6"

Clamp

In this position, the wedge-shaped stop on this shooting board holds the stock vertically for unimpeded edge-jointing of narrow stock.

Flip the fixture over to joint edges of thin stock. The plane's side uses the bench as a reference surface to ensure a square cut.

# Multipurpose Shooting Board
Hold work firmly to plane edges true.

Partnered with a sharp plane, this two-faced fixture successfully joints the boards that your power jointer shouldn't touch. If you do a lot of work with small pieces, or have a workbench with a top that isn't perfectly flat, investing a few minutes to make this fixture will be time well spent.

Use the top face for narrow stock. The wedge holds stock for jointing without additional clamps or stops. Simply position the stock between the fixed blocks and tap the wedge to lock the stock in place (**Photo A**).

Flip the fixture over, and the bottom cleat doubles as a stop for edge-shooting thin boards. Butt the stock against the cleat and shoot the edge, as shown in **Photo B**.

The fixture's dimensions aren't critical, but in order for it to work properly, the edges of the base must be perfectly straight.

## FIGURE 1
Multipurpose Shooting Jig

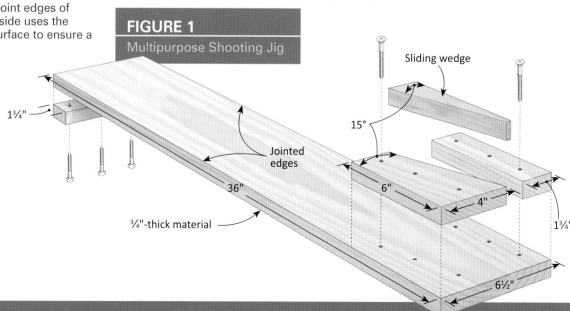

Sliding wedge

15°

Jointed edges

1¾"

36"

¾"-thick material

6"

4"

1¾"

6½"

# CHAPTER 4

# BENCHES AND TABLES

## On-Demand Folding Table
### For your home or shop.

I t's easy to imagine this table brimming with enough snacks to last you through the big game on TV. But it can also be a great helper in the workshop, holding tools or materials to keep your workbench clutter-free. Best of all, the table folds in a flash so it doesn't take up valuable space when you're not using it. Making one table is a good idea, but building a set of four—or more—multiplies their value throughout your house.

### Start with the legs and cleats

**1** Rip blanks 1½" wide for the legs (A) and cleats (B) from ¾" stock. Referring to **Figure 1** on page 69, mark the finished length of each piece with a 60° angle. Use your mitersaw or table saw to make the angled cuts. Set up a stop block to ensure identical lengths.

**2** Mark the radius on the opposite end of each leg (A) and cleat (B) with your compass. As you do that, you'll also be marking the center point of one hole in each piece. Measuring from the end of each leg (A), mark the center point of the second hole.

**3** Drill the holes with a ¾" brad-point bit chucked into your drill press, as shown in **Photo A** (page 68). With a fresh backing board under the workpiece and a moderate feed rate, you'll virtually eliminate tear-out. (See the **Convenience-Plus Buying Guide** on page 70 for ordering info on a brad-point bit as well as a Forstner bit, an excellent alternative.)

## FIGURE 1

NOTE: For the items needed to make the table, see the **Convenience-Plus Buying Guide** on page 70. Also, refer to the handy **Cut List** (page 70).

## FIGURE 2

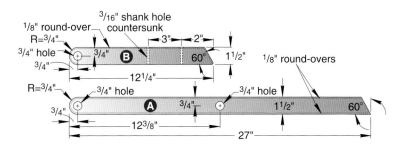

**4** Referring to **Figure 1**, measure and mark the holes in the edge of each cleat (B). At your drill press, drill and countersink these holes. See the **Convenience-Plus Buying Guide** on page 70 for a smooth-cutting single-flute countersink for #10 screws.

**5** Cut the ¾" radius on each leg (A) and cleat (B). Use your bandsaw to cut just to the waste side of the line, and smooth the radius with your disk sander.

**6** Rout ⅛" round-overs along the edges indicated on **Figure 1**. Be sure to round over both faces of each piece. Note that there's no round-over along the edges of the cleats (B) that will be next to the top (D). For maximum convenience and control, chuck the round-over bit into your table-mounted router. Sand the legs to final smoothness and slightly ease any edges without round-overs.

### Make the stretchers and cut the dowels

**1** Rip and crosscut the stretchers (C) to the size in the **Cut List** on page 70.

**2** Drill the screw shank holes in the stretchers (C) where shown in **Figure 2**. For the best appearance, use your drill press to countersink these holes identically.

**3** Cut the ¾" dowel to the lengths shown on **Figure 3**. Note that you'll need two pieces 1½" long. Don't sand the dowels at this time. You'll want a snug fit where the dowels are glued to the legs (A).

Clamping a stop block to the drill-press table makes it easy to position parts for identical hole location.

### TIP ALERT

Another way to eliminate tear-out is to drill until the tip of the brad-point bit just breaks through the bottom face of the workpiece. Flip the piece and complete the hole from the opposite face.

### TIP ALERT

Most table saw miter gauges read 90° for a right-angle crosscut. In that case, set the gauge to 60° to make the angle on the legs and cleats. But mitersaws (and a few table saw miter gauges) read 0° at the crosscut position. In that case, you'll set the gauge to 30° for the cut.

## FIGURE 3

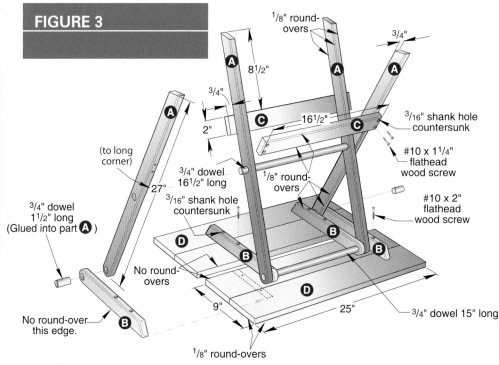

## Make the top

**1** Make the two-piece top as a slightly oversized one-piece panel. As shown in **Photo B**, I had a wide board tht I used in the center of the 19" wide glue-up. Arrange the boards you have for the best-looking grain match. Allow the panel to dry overnight then remove the clamps and scrape away any glue squeeze out. Cut a square end, then crosscut the panel to length. Finally, set your tablesaw fence to 9" wide and rip the panel in half to create the two-piece top.

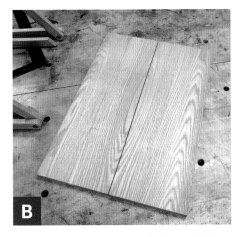

Positioning a wide board in the middle of the panel then sawing apart the two-part top after glue-up effectively camouflages the folding joint.

**2** Rout the round-overs along the outside edges as shown in **Figure 3**. Note that you don't rout the edges or ends where the two halves butt against each other.

**3** Sand the top up to 220-grit, being careful to maintain a crisp edge where the two halves meet. Lightly "break" these edges with your sanding block to help prevent splintering.

## Begin the assembly

**1** Start with one leg (A) and the two long dowels to begin assembling the inner pair of legs. Wipe glue inside the end hole, and press in the 15"-long dowel until its end is flush with the outer face of the leg. Wipe glue inside the other hole, and press in the 16½" dowel until its end is ¾" past the outer face of the leg.

**2** Add two cleats (B) to the 15" dowel, referring to **Figure 3** to ensure that the angles on the cleats (B) match the leg (A).

**3** Wipe glue inside the holes of a leg (A), and position the angle on its end to match those already assembled. Again, press the end of the 15" dowel flush with the face of the leg, and the end of the 16½" dowel ¾" past the face of the leg. Remove excess glue from both ends of the 16½" dowel.

Carefully squaring the leg assembly will help ensure that your table sits solidly and folds smoothly.

**4** Add the remaining legs (A) to the assembly, placing them on the 16½" dowel. Referring to **Figure 3**, you'll see that the end angle of these legs is opposite those already assembled.

**5** Lay the assembly flat on your bench, and position the inside frame stretcher (C) 8½" from the lower tip of the inner legs. The inside frame stretcher has its holes 1⅛" from the ends, and it overhangs the outer frame legs. Next, square the stretcher as shown in **Photo C**. Ensure that the distance between the legs is consistent from end to end.

**6** Drill ⅛" pilot holes into the legs, using the shank holes in the stretcher (C) as guides, as shown in **Photo D** on page 70. Attach the stretcher to the legs with four #10 x 1¼" screws.

**7** Turn over the leg assembly, and fasten the outside frame stretcher (C) in a similar manner. Check that the assembly is square and there's an even gap between the legs.

**8** Glue a short dowel into the end hole of each outer leg so that the stub points outward from the assembly. Add a cleat (B) to each dowel, referring to **Figure 3** for proper placement.

**D**

Drilling pilot holes into the legs helps ensure that driving the screws won't split the lumber.

## Square the leg assembly and add the top

**1** Put the top halves (E) face down on your bench. Make sure that the edges are flush.

**2** Align the angled leg ends with a framing square as shown in **Photo E**. Open the leg assembly until the square sits parallel to the bottoms of the legs. Clamp the assembly to keep it from slipping and center it on the top with a combination square.

**3** Drill ⅛" pilot holes into the top. Use a masking tape "flag" on your drill bit to help make sure that you don't drill too deeply. Drive eight #10 x 2" screws through the cleats and into the top.

**E**

## Convenience-Plus Buying Guide

| | |
|---|---|
| ☐ 1 | ¾" Brad-Point Drill Bit |
| ☐ 2 | ¾" Forstner Drill Bit |
| ☐ 3 | Woodcraft Roundover Bit, ⅛" Radius, ¼" Shank |
| ☐ 4 | ¾"-Dia Oak Dowel, 36" |
| ☐ 5 | Single-Flute Countersink For #10 Screws |
| ☐ 6 | Watco Danish Oil, 1 Qt |
| ☐ 7 | General Arm-R-Seal, 1 Qt |

## On-Demand Folding Table Cut List

| | PART | THICKNESS | WIDTH | LENGTH | QTY. | MAT'L |
|---|---|---|---|---|---|---|
| A | Legs | ¾" | 1½" | 27" | 4 | Red Oak |
| B | Cleats | ¾" | 1½" | 12¼" | 4 | Red Oak |
| C | Stretcher | ¾" | 2" | 16½" | 2 | Red Oak |
| D* | Top (half) | ¾" | 9" | 25" | 2 | Red Oak |
| | Short Dowel | ¾" | ¾" | 1½" | 2 | Red Oak |
| | Top Dowel | ¾" | ¾" | 15" | 1 | Red Oak |
| | Bottom Dowel | ¾" | ¾" | 16½" | 1 | Red Oak |

\* Indicates a part that is initially cut larger than this final dimension; please see the instructions for further details.

## Cutting Diagram

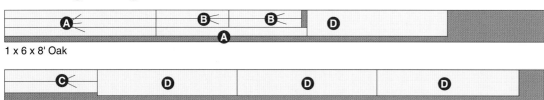

1 x 6 x 8' Oak

1 x 6 x 8' Oak

OVERALL DIMENSIONS | 51"w × 36"d × 36"h

## Adjustable 3-in-1 Assembly Table

Drop leaves and a built-in jack provide loads of options.

If your workbench and table saw too often serve as the place you glue up frames, boxes, and other small to medium projects, why not free them up with a dedicated assembly surface? This mobile table, made from two ¾"-thick sheets of MDF and maple trim, provides assembly surfaces in three sizes, with the largest measuring 36 × 51" when both drop leaves are raised. A scissor jack cleverly mounted inside (see **Figure 3** on page 74), along with four star knobs, lets you lock in the desired working height from 24" to 36". This adjustable feature also allows the project to function as a precision outfeed table or benchtop power tool stand. When not in use, drop the leaves and roll the table against the wall or below a table saw wing. *Note: See the* **Convenience-Plus Buying Guide** *on page 77 for the products used in this story. You'll certainly want the jack on hand during construction.*

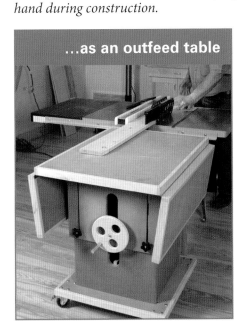

...as an outfeed table

...as a benchtop toolstand

### Build the inner sleeve first

**1** Cut the inner sleeve ends (A), sides (B), jack supports (C), and support plate (D) to the overall sizes in the **Cut List** on page 78. Also see the **Cutting Diagram** on page 77.

**2** Chuck a 2½" Forstner bit in your drill press and bore holes where shown in the parts view for inner sleeve ends (A) in **Figure 1** on page 72.

**3** Strike lines for the jack slots referring to **Figure 3** and cut out the waste as shown in **Photo A**. Use a rasp or curved sanding block to clean up the sawn slots, then rout a ⅛" round-over along both faces of the slot.

**4** Clamp the two jack supports (C) face-to-face, aligning the edges and ends. Mark the location of the centered ¾ × 3½" notches on one face. While the supports are still clamped together, cut the notches in both pieces. Separate the two and test the fit, as shown in **Figure 3** on page 74. Adjust as needed with a rasp.

**5** Using a pocket-hole jig, drill five evenly-spaced holes along the inside faces of the inner sleeve sides (B) at the ends, as shown in **Photo B**, and of parts A and B where shown in **Figure 1**. Drill pocket holes in one jack support (C) in order to attach it to the inner sleeve. (Don't own a pocket-hole jig? Join the ends and sides with simple butt joints held together with glue and 5mm × 40mm Confirmat screws. See the Alternate Joinery Detail in **Figure 3**.)

**6** Rout centered and intersecting ¾" dadoes ¼" deep on the bottom face of support plate (D) to fit jack supports (C) where shown in **Figure 1**.

**7** Drill the pilot holes and then screw the inner sleeve sides (B) to ends (A), aligning the top and bottom edges as shown in **Photo C**. Clamp parts in place to ensure control during assembly and check for square.

**8** Center the jack support (C) with the pocket holes (slot up) in the inner sleeve assembly. Use the other slotted jack support (C) to center and secure the piece in place while driving the screws. Ensure that it's flush with the bottom edges of the sleeve assembly. Now drive the screws. Slip the remaining jack support onto the fixed support. Square the support assembly with the support plate (D) as shown in **Photo D** and secure it with Confirmat screws. (Note: You'll need to unscrew the plate later in order to fasten the lower sleeve to the base.)

## FIGURE 1
### Router Mortising Jig

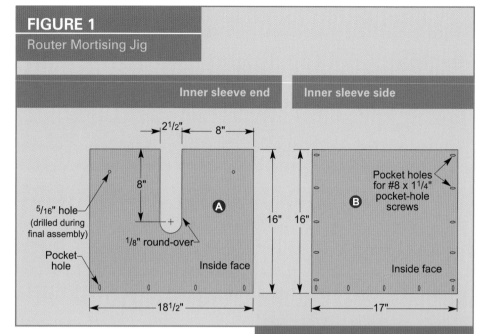

Inner sleeve end

Inner sleeve side

2½"   8"

8"

5/16" hole (drilled during final assembly)

ⓐ

1/8" round-over

Pocket hole

Inside face

16"   16"

Pocket holes for #8 x 1¼" pocket-hole screws

ⓑ

Inside face

18½"

17"

#### Support plate

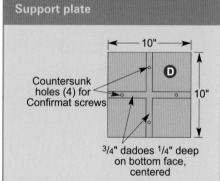

10"

ⓓ

Countersunk holes (4) for Confirmat screws

10"

¾" dadoes ¼" deep on bottom face, centered

## TIP ALERT

Use Confirmat screws when joining MDF or particleboard parts. Their special thread design reduces stripping out pilot holes and splitting the edges of parts.

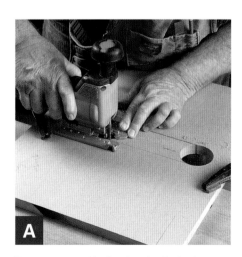

**A** Bore centered holes for the jack slots through the inner sleeve ends. Cut out the waste with a jigsaw.

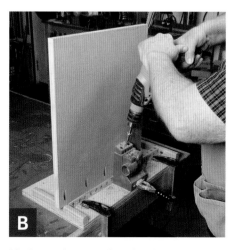

**B** Mark evenly spaced pocket holes on the face of the workpiece, and then use the stepped bit to drill the pocket holes.

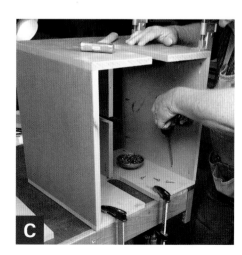

**C** Using an extended square-drive bit in a portable drill, drive #8 × 1¼" screws into the pockets and joining parts.

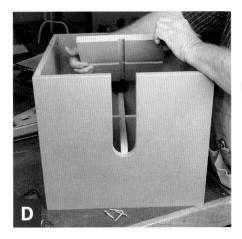

**D** Locate the dadoes of the support plate onto the jack supports. Lock them in place with Confirmat screws.

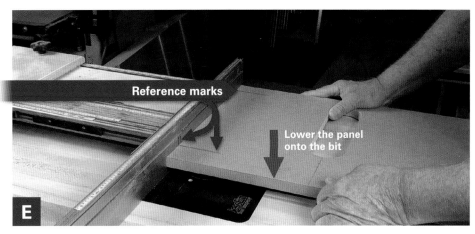

Reference marks

Lower the panel onto the bit

**E** With the workpiece snug to the fence, lower the outer sleeve ends over the hidden bit using the alignment lines as a guide. Well-placed reference lines for the bit edges and slot ends let you accurately rout matching slots.

**9** Face-glue and plane enough stock for a 2"-thick block. Crosscut and rip the lamination to 3⅜ × 6" for the jack's top plate (E). Drill a ⅝"- diameter hole ½" deep where shown in the **Top Plate Detail** in **Figure 3** on page 74. Apply a 3"-wide piece of Slick Strip on the top face. From ¼" plywood scrap, make a 2"-wide spacer (F) like the one in the detail. Insert the lag screw through the jack and spacer and fasten it to the top plate, allowing for a little play when raising or lowering the outer sleeve.

### Now build the outer sleeve

**1** Cut outer sleeve ends (G) and sides (H) to size plus ⅛" wider than the dimensions in the **Cut List**. Locate the vertical center of each end (G) and strike a line from top to bottom. Mark the 2½" hole locations on the parts and drill the holes with a Forstner bit. Jigsaw out the waste, smooth the sawn edges, and rout ⅛" round-overs where shown in **Figure 2**.

**2** Chuck a ⅜" straight bit (with a 1" cut length) in your table-mounted router, raise it ¼", adjust the fence to cut the slots in the ends (G) where shown in **Figure 2**. Next, mark the locations of the bit edges on the fence and the top and bottom ends of the slots on the workpiece. Turn on the router,

align the left-hand slot reference line with the left-hand bit location reference line, and lower the workpiece onto the bit as shown in **Photo E**. Move the workpiece from right to left until the right-hand slot line and bit line align. Do this for all four slots. Now, remove the workpieces, raise the bit another ¼", and repeat. Raise the bit again until you've cut through the workpieces, creating all four slots.

**3** Apply ¾"-wide adhesive-backed Slick Strips 1" in from the inside edges (**Photo F**, page 74) and a second set 3¼" in. See **Figure 2**. The strips allow the outer sleeve to easily slide over the inner sleeve when raising and lowering the jack.

## FIGURE 2
### Outer Sleeve Parts View

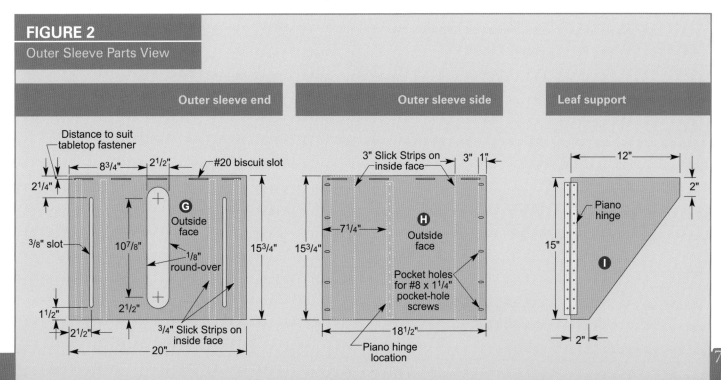

**Outer sleeve end**

Distance to suit tabletop fastener

8¾"  2½"  #20 biscuit slot

2¼"

⅜" slot

10⅞"

**G** Outside face

⅛" round-over

15¾"

1½"

2½"

¾" Slick Strips on inside face

2½"

20"

**Outer sleeve side**

3" Slick Strips on inside face  3"  1"

15¾"

7¼"

**H** Outside face

Pocket holes for #8 x 1¼" pocket-hole screws

18½"

Piano hinge location

**Leaf support**

12"  2"

Piano hinge

15

**I**

2"

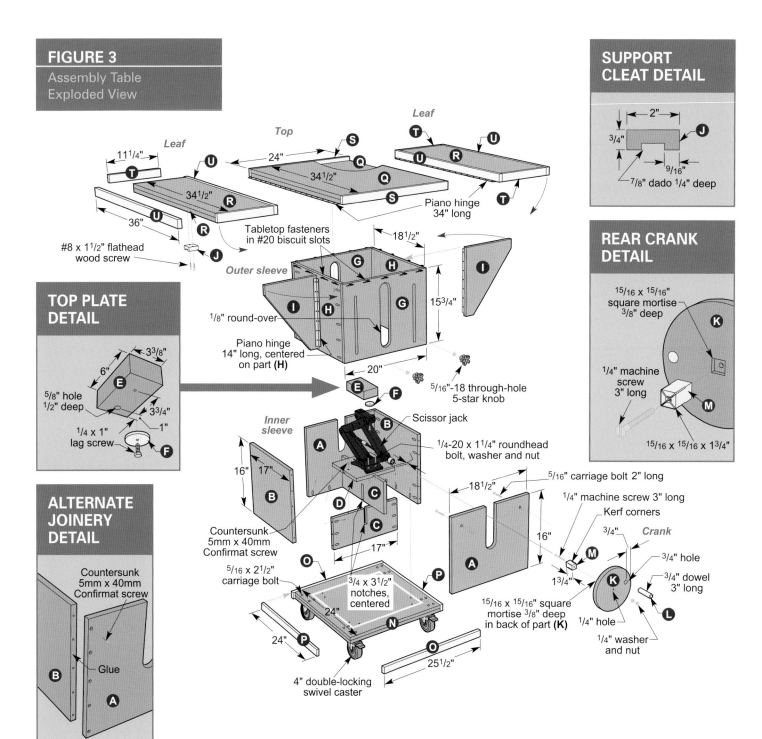

## FIGURE 3
Assembly Table
Exploded View

**Leaf**

11¹/₄"

**T**

**Top**

**S**

**Q**

24"

34¹/₂"

**Q**

**Leaf**

**T**

**U**

**U**

**R**

**U**

34¹/₂"

**R**

**S**

36"

**U**

**R**

**J**

#8 x 1¹/₂" flathead wood screw

Tabletop fasteners in #20 biscuit slots

Piano hinge 34" long

**SUPPORT CLEAT DETAIL**

2"

3/4"

**J**

9/16"

7/8" dado 1/4" deep

**Outer sleeve**

18¹/₂"

**G**

**H**

**I**

**I**

**H**

**G**

15³/₄"

1/8" round-over

Piano hinge 14" long, centered on part (H)

20"

**E**

**F**

5/16"-18 through-hole 5-star knob

**TOP PLATE DETAIL**

3³/₈"

6"

**E**

5/8" hole 1/2" deep

3³/₄"

1/4 x 1" lag screw

1"

**F**

**REAR CRANK DETAIL**

15/16 x 15/16" square mortise 3/8" deep

**K**

1/4" machine screw 3" long

**M**

15/16 x 15/16 x 1³/₄"

**Inner sleeve**

**A**

**B**

Scissor jack

1/4-20 x 1¹/₄" roundhead bolt, washer and nut

16"

17"

**B**

**D**

**C**

Countersunk 5mm x 40mm Confirmat screw

**C**

18¹/₂"

5/16" carriage bolt 2" long

1/4" machine screw 3" long

Kerf corners

**ALTERNATE JOINERY DETAIL**

Countersunk 5mm x 40mm Confirmat screw

5/16 x 2¹/₂" carriage bolt

**O**

17"

3/4 x 3¹/₂" notches, centered

**P**

**A**

16"

**M**

3/4"

**Crank**

3/4" hole

3/4" dowel 3" long

**K**

1³/₄"

15/16 x 15/16" square mortise 3/8" deep in back of part (K)

1/4" hole

**L**

1/4" washer and nut

**B**

Glue

**A**

24"

24"

**P**

**N**

**O**

4" double-locking swivel caster

25¹/₂"

**4** Clamp the outer sleeve ends (G) to the inner sleeve, aligning the jack slots. Hold the sides (H) to the ends and mark the cutline for trimming the sides to exact width as shown in **Photo G**. Trim the sides to finished size.

**5** Drill pocket holes along the ends of the outer sleeve sides (H) on the outside faces, then vertically apply 3"-wide Slick Strips to the inside faces 1" in from the edge. (See **Figure 2**.)

**F**

Press the Slick Strips in place with a laminate roller or a block of wood, bevel-cutting the ends.

Inside face

**G**

Hold the outer sleeve sides to the clamped ends to get a precise width measurement.

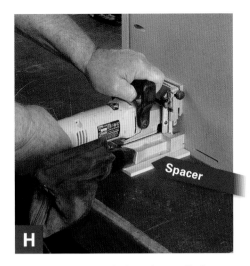

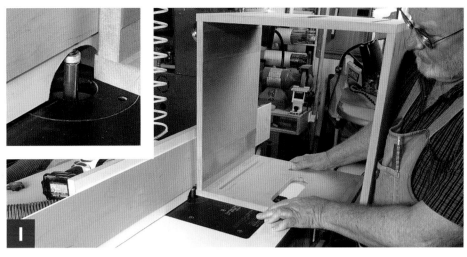

Place a ¼" spacer below the tool's base and adjust the cutter for a #20 biscuit slot. Make the cut.

Place the outer sleeve on the router table and trim off the waste along the edges with a flush-trim bit.

**6** Fit outer sides (H) snugly against the inner sleeve and clamp them in place, flushing the bottom edges on a flat surface. Now, drive the pocketscrews. Undo the clamps, and slide the fastened outer sleeve up and off the inner sleeve. (You may need to clamp a caul across the top of the outer sleeve and use the jack to raise the sleeves.) With the two sleeves separated, apply a liberal coat of wax to the outside faces of the inner sleeve.

**7** With the outer sleeve upside-down on a bench or table surface, cut biscuit slots to accommodate the tabletop fasteners used to hold the top in place as shown in **Photo H**. Use a tabletop fastener to determine the distance from the top edge for the biscuit slots. Ours measured ⅝".

**8** Adhere a ¼"-thick length of scrap plywood to your router-table fence for clearance, chuck a flush-trim bit in the router, adjust the fence for a clean flush-trim cut, and rout the waste from the outer sleeve ends (**Photo I** and **inset**).

**9** Cut two leaf supports (I) to the size and shape in **Figure 2**. Using a router table and straight bit or dado blade, cut a ¾"-plus groove ¼" deep in a ¾ × 2 × 12" piece of maple. From it, cut two 2"-long support cleats (J). Drill screw holes in the cleats. (See **Figure 3**.) Set both I and J parts aside for later.

**10** Make the crank handwheel (K), handle (L), and shaft (M) for the crank assembly using the dimensions in the **Cut List** and **Figure 3**. Drill the holes and glue the dowel handle into the handwheel. Handsaw intersecting kerfs at the corners ¾" in from one end of the square shaft and drill a countersunk ¼" hole through the length. Set aside.

### Construct the wheeled base

**1** Crosscut a 24½" piece of MDF from one end of a full sheet. Next, crosscut that piece into two pieces that roughly measure 24½" square. (See the **Cutting Diagram**.) Now, apply glue to the mating faces and face-join the two squares together, aligning factory edges. Clamp and weight the pieces together and let dry.

**2** Working from the factory edges, cut the workpiece square on the table saw, trimming all four edges to achieve a 24"-square part to create the base (N).

**3** Rip enough maple stock for the base side and end bands (O, P) to 1⅝" wide. Now cut, glue, and clamp the pieces along the edges using butt or miter joints as desired. Once the glue dries, flush-trim the edges of the bands with the base. Rout a ⅛" round-over on all maple edges.

**4** Place the casters just inside the bands (O, P) on the base (N) and mark the hole locations for the hardware. Drill the holes through the base, but do not attach the casters at this time.

**5** Place the base assembly on a work surface. Now center and clamp the inner sleeve to the base and screw it in place as shown in **Photo J**, using the pocket holes drilled earlier.

To prevent bulging the inner sleeve, secure it to the base with clamped cauls. Remove plate (D) to access pocket holes.

**6** Slip the outer sleeve over the inner sleeve, flush the top edges, and clamp it in place. Now, drill $\frac{5}{16}$" holes through the inner sleeve, using the top end of the $\frac{3}{8}$"-wide slots as a guide. Insert 2½" carriage bolts through the holes from the inside, and then add $\frac{5}{16}$" fender washers and star knobs. Tighten the knobs to sink the carriage bolt heads into the MDF.

Avoid stripping out the screw holes by using a manual screwdriver to drive the hinge screws.

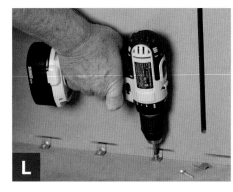

With the outer sleeve centered on the top assembly, screw the tabletop fasteners in place.

### Add the top, leaves, and leaf supports

**1** Crosscut the remaining piece of MDF into two equal 3'-wide halves. Apply glue to both mating faces and clamp and weight the pieces together, flushing the factory edges. (Refer to **Figure 3** and the **Cutting Diagram**.) As with the base, use the factory edge to rip the panel to 35" wide. Now run the long cut edge against the fence and then trim the glue-up to a finished width of 34½".

**2** Set your table saw fence 1⅝" from the blade and rip enough ¾"-thick maple band material for all four edges of the top (Q) and two leaves (R), cutting two of the pieces to 50" long. Center, glue, and clamp the 50"-pieces to the long edges of the glue-up panel. Once dry, flush-trim the maple and flush-cut the waste from the ends of the maple bands.

**3** Using your table saw and miter gauge with an auxiliary fence or a circular saw with a straightedge, cut one end of the banded panel to 11¾" wide and set aside. Next, cut the top (Q) to 24" wide and set it aside. With the remaining piece, cut one of two leaves (R) to the final 11¼" width, running the long sawn edge against the fence. Doing the same, return to the 11¾"-wide piece and trim it to final width for the other leaf (R).

**4** Cut the six remaining pieces for the top and leaf end bands (U), glue and clamp them in place, and flush-trim as described before. Label the top surface for the top and leaf assemblies.

**5** Ease the hard edges of the top and leaf assemblies, except where the hinges attach, with a handheld router and ⅛" round-over bit.

**6** Cut the continuous hinges to 35¾". Place the top and leaves bottom face up on a flat work surface. Place $1/16$" spacers between the leaves and top (to provide clearance for the leaf supports [I]), align the edges, locate the hinge, and drill pilot holes for the screws. (We used a Vix bit to ensure centered holes.) Now drive the screws. See **Figure 4** for reference.

**FIGURE 4**
Assembly Table
Side View

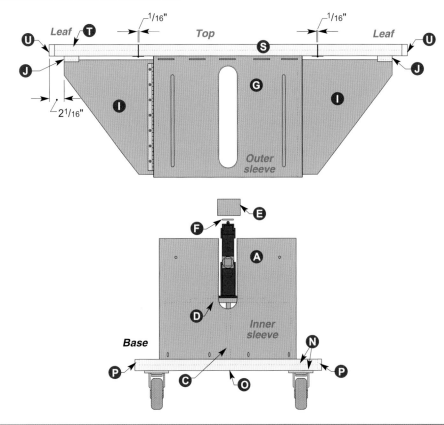

**7** Drill four holes at the corners through the base of the jack. Bolt the jack and accompanying top plate (E) to the support plate (D). Now, using a helper, turn the sleeve and base assembly upside down and centered on the top assembly. Insert the tabletop fasteners in the biscuit slots and screw them to the top.

**8** Carefully attach the cut-off pieces of continuous hinge from Step 7 to each leaf support (I) exactly as shown in **Figure 2.** Strike a vertical line 7¼" in from one edge of the outside sleeve on parts H. Retrieve a support cleat (J) and fit it on the outside top edge of one leaf support (I). Rest both parts on the bottom face of the leaf (R) and align the unhinged face of the leaf support with the vertical line. Drill the pilot holes and drive the screws. (When the leaf supports are folded, you want the outside ends to be flush with the corners of the outer sleeve.)

Repeat this procedure for the other leaf support, offsetting it to the diagonal corner.

**9** Screw the centered support cleats (J) in place on the leaves (R).

**10** Install the casters to the base with carriage bolts, washers, and nuts, and then solicit a helper to carefully stand the assembly table upright on the floor.

**11** Chisel a ¹⁵⁄₁₆" square mortise ⅜" deep in the handwheel center and drill a centered ¼" hole in it. Glue the unkerfed end of the square shaft (M) into handwheel (K). Next insert a 3"-long ¼-20 flathead machine screw through the kerfed end of the square shaft (M) and that end into the square opening in the jack. Add the washer, tighten the nut, and hacksaw the screw to length. Cut a screwdriver slot in the cut-off end of the screw. By tightening the nut, you'll spread the shaft in the jack opening, locking it in place. You may need the slot to hold the screw while tightening the nut. Now give your completed assembly table a test ride up and down. Provide a clear finish if desired.

## Cutting Diagram

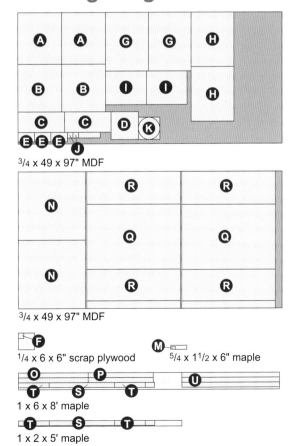

¾ x 49 x 97" MDF

¾ x 49 x 97" MDF

¼ x 6 x 6" scrap plywood

⁵⁄₄ x 1½ x 6" maple

1 x 6 x 8' maple

1 x 2 x 5' maple

## Convenience-Plus Buying Guide

# Assembly Table Cut List

| | PART | THICKNESS | WIDTH | LENGTH | QTY. | MAT'L |
|---|---|---|---|---|---|---|
| **Inner sleeve** | | | | | | |
| A | Inner sleeve ends | ¾" | 18½" | 16" | 2 | MDF |
| B | Inner sleeve sides | ¾" | 17" | 16" | 2 | MDF |
| C | Jack supports | ¾" | 7⅜" | 17" | 2 | MDF |
| D | Support plate | ¾" | 10" | 10" | 1 | MDF |
| E | Top plate | 2" | 3⅜" | 6" | 1 | MDF |
| F | Spacer | ¼" | 2" | 2" | 1 | PLY |
| **Outer sleeve** | | | | | | |
| G* | Outer sleeve ends | ¾" | 20" | 15¾" | 2 | MDF |
| H* | Outer sleeve sides | ¾" | 18½" | 15¾" | 2 | MDF |
| I | Leaf supports | ¾" | 12" | 15" | 2 | MDF |
| J | Support cleats | ¾" | 2" | 2" | 2 | MDF |
| K | Handwheel | ¾" | 8" dia. | | 1 | LBP |
| L | Handle | ¾" dia. | | 3" | 1 | HD |
| M | Shaft | 15/16" | 15/16" | 1¾" | 1 | M |
| **Base** | | | | | | |
| N | Base | 1½" | 24" | 24" | 1 | MDF |
| O* | Side edge bands | ¾" | 1½" | 25½" | 2 | M |
| P* | End edge bands | ¾" | 1½" | 24" | 2 | M |
| **Top assembly** | | | | | | |
| Q | Top | 1½" | 24" | 34½" | 1 | MDF |
| R | Leaves | 1½" | 11¼" | 34½" | 2 | MDF |
| S* | Top side bands | ¾" | 1½" | 24" | 2 | M |
| T* | Leaf side bands | ¾" | 1½" | 11¼" | 4 | M |
| U | Top and leaf end bands | ¾" | 1½" | 36" | 6 | M |

**Materials:** MDF=Medium-Density Fiberboard; PLY=Plywood; HD=Hardwood Dowel;
    M=Maple; LBP=Laminated Birch Plywood
**Supplies:** #8 × 1½" and #8 × 2" FH wood screws, #8 × ¾" and #14 × 1¼" panhead screws,
    ¼-20 × 1¼" RH bolts, ¼" hex nuts, and ¼" flat washers.
*    Parts are cut larger and then trimmed to size during construction. See instructions.

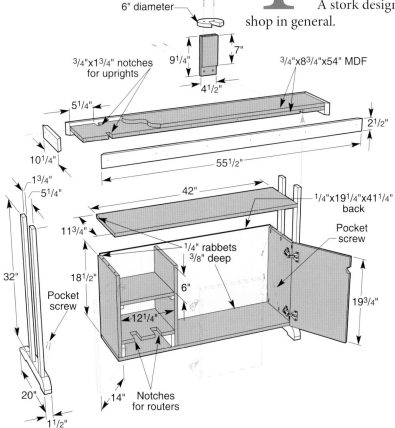

## FIGURE 1
### Dovetail Jig Workbench

# Dovetail Jig Workbench

T his design includes a base that supports the 24" Porter-Cable Omnijig. A stork design adds texture and interest to the cabinet doors and the shop in general.

6" diameter

³/₄"x1³/₄" notches for uprights

9¹/₄"    7"

4¹/₂"

³/₄"x8³/₄"x54" MDF

5¹/₄"

2¹/₂"

10¹/₄"

55¹/₂"

1³/₄"

5¹/₄"

42"

¹/₄"x19¹/₄"x41¹/₄" back

11³/₄"

Pocket screw

¹/₄" rabbets ³/₈" deep

32"

18¹/₂"

6"

Pocket screw

19³/₄"

12¹/₄"

20"

14"    Notches for routers

1¹/₂"

## Lazy-Susan Finishing Table

**T**his design takes advantage of the time-saving convenience of spray-finishing. To ensure consistent results, simply rotate the table to rotate the work, so you can easily maintain a consistent distance to the surface. A 9" lazy-Susan bearing offers good stability and smooth action, even under heavy loads.

### FIGURE 1
Lazy-Susan Finishing Table

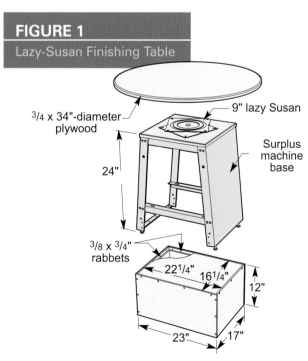

$3/4$ x 34"-diameter plywood

9" lazy Susan

Surplus machine base

24"

$3/8$ x $3/4$" rabbets

$22 1/4$"  $16 1/4$"  12"

23"  17"

Partner up square dogs and small wedges to join thin stock. Waxed paper prevents the panel from sticking.

Slide the workpiece into the hook to lock it in place. Tap the wedge's small end to release the vise-like grip.

# Planing Stops, Dogs, and Wedges
Accessorize your bench for special tasks.

**A** good vise is only half the equation. In order to catch and hold, you'll need a few flexible points to clamp against. (If your bench doesn't have dog holes, it's time to reach for your drill. Make two parallel rows of ¾"-diameter holes along your bench's front edge and a perpendicular row aligned with your end vise. Space the holes 6" apart.)

Planing stops are plain simple. They're nothing more than ⅜"-thick wood strips studded with a pair of dowels sized and spaced to fit the bench. The stop's thickness leaves enough wood to achieve a decent glue joint with the dowel, but doesn't usually interfere when planing thin stock. (When planing or scraping thinner material, place your work on top of a piece of ⅛"-thick hardboard.)

Dogs, or single-dowel stops, come next. I rank them just under planing stops because they don't work well without a partner such as a stop, vise, or another dog. For planing or scraping, a planing stop works well enough on its own.

The dogs show why round dog holes have the edge over square holes. The round studs allow the heads to rotate and automatically find clamping points on parts that don't line up with the vise. This rotational advantage comes into full play when teamed with a wedge. As shown in **Photo A**, the combo can replace clamps for delicate glue-ups.

A larger wedged stop can be a simple but effective substitute for a vise, especially when dressing small parts (**Photo B**). In addition to providing an instantaneous grip, the stop uses the top as backup so that the stock doesn't bend when planing, scraping, or sanding.

To make a wedged stop, fit a planing stop diagonally across your bench and then work out the angle on a piece of cardboard before transferring the pattern onto ⅜"-thick plywood.

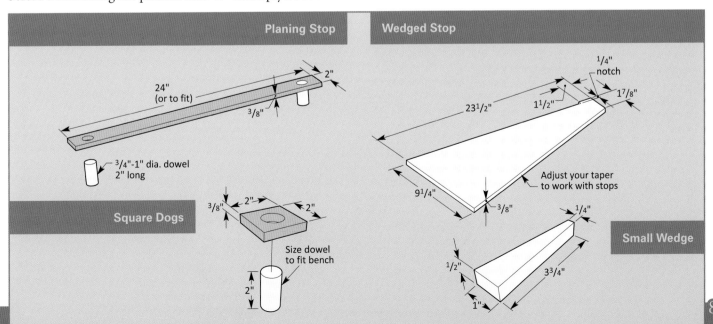

**Planing Stop**

24" (or to fit) — 2" — 3/8"

3/4"-1" dia. dowel 2" long

**Square Dogs**

3/8" — 2" — 2"

Size dowel to fit bench — 2"

**Wedged Stop**

1/4" notch — 1 7/8"

23 1/2" — 1 1/2"

9 1/4" — 3/8"

Adjust your taper to work with stops

**Small Wedge**

1/4" — 1/2" — 3 3/4" — 1"

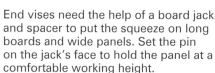

End vises need the help of a board jack and spacer to put the squeeze on long boards and wide panels. Set the pin on the jack's face to hold the panel at a comfortable working height.

## TIP ALERT

Quick-drying shellac is a perfect jig and fixture finish. Wax can be useful, but go lightly. A little can help lubricate a sticking dowel; too much will cause accessories to slide around your bench.

## Board Jacks and Vise Spacers
### Make your bench work even better.

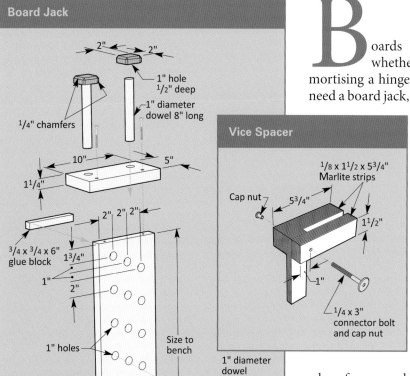

**Board Jack**

2"  2"
1" hole
1/2" deep
1" diameter
dowel 8" long
1/4" chamfers
10"  5"
1 1/4"
2"  2"  2"
3/4 x 3/4 x 6" glue block
1 3/4"
1"
2"
1" holes
Size to bench
1 1/4"
1" diameter dowel 5" long
3 1/4" x 1" I.D. vinyl tubing
8"
#8 x 3 1/2" flathead wood screw
1" chamfer
3 x 3 x 12" base

**Vice Spacer**

1/8 x 1 1/2 x 5 3/4" Marlite strips
Cap nut
5 3/4"
1 1/2"
1"
1/4 x 3" connector bolt and cap nut

**B**oards and panels usually require some edge work, whether it's planing off burns or saw marks, jointing, or mortising a hinge. To make full use of the front of your bench you need a board jack, a solid point to rest the free end of your workpiece so that you can grab the other end with your vise. Jacks come in almost as many flavors as workbenches, but most fall into two categories: built-ins that slide along the front and after-the-facts that clamp into a tail vise. The first work well with short boards, but it's hard to justify the retro-work involved in such an upgrade.

My jack is easier than a major retrofit, but like a "slider," it moves easily along the front of your bench and works independently of an end vise. Made from cheap 2× and 4× stock, the jack stands in the corner when not in use.

Use the figure as a guide, but note that you'll need to adjust the height of the face so that the head fits under your benchtop. Drill the pin holes so that the face of the jig sits flush with the front edge of your workbench.

Sometimes one fixture leads to the next. When I first put the jack to use, the wide jawed vise racked (the open end closed more than the other); consequently, it failed to provide the necessary grip. This self-setting vise spacer (**Inset**) solved the problem. To use the spacer "sandwich," set it on the opposite end of your vise. As the jaws open, the strips will fall into the gap.

# Downdraft Sanding Table

If your shop doesn't have room for this full-scale downdraft table, consider half-sizing the lengths of the top and base for a better fit. You could even omit the legs, creating a unit to place atop your workbench or sawhorses when needed and then compactly stow to conserve space. Abrasives and finishing supplies fill the shelves underneath.

**FIGURE 1**
Downdraft Sanding Table

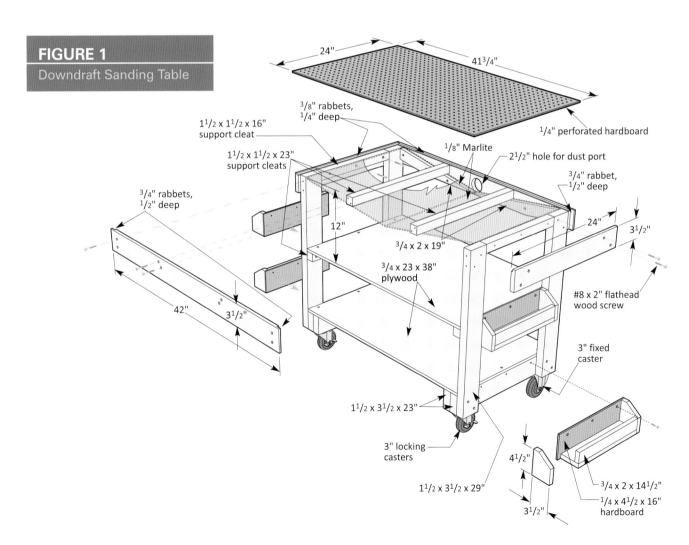

24"
41³/₄"

¹/₄" perforated hardboard

³/₈" rabbets, ¹/₄" deep

1¹/₂ x 1¹/₂ x 16" support cleat

1¹/₂ x 1¹/₂ x 23" support cleats

¹/₈" Marlite

2¹/₂" hole for dust port

³/₄" rabbet, ¹/₂" deep

³/₄" rabbets, ¹/₂" deep

12"

24"

3¹/₂"

³/₄ x 2 x 19"

³/₄ x 23 x 38" plywood

#8 x 2" flathead wood screw

42"

3¹/₂"

3" fixed caster

1¹/₂ x 3¹/₂ x 23"

3" locking casters

1¹/₂ x 3¹/₂ x 29"

4¹/₂"

3¹/₂"

³/₄ x 2 x 14¹/₂"

¹/₄ x 4¹/₂ x 16" hardboard

## Auxiliary Workbench
Add a second level for close-in assignments.

Build an auxiliary workbench to sit on top of your woodworking bench. It's much easier on the back than bending over the typical height bench, and it lets you keep delicate work closer to eye level. The bench raises the working surface just over 10", allowing you to stand comfortably when routing grooves and doing string inlay, as well as other meticulous tasks.

Edge-joined 1¼"-thick maple makes up the top, along with breadboard ends to allow for expansion and contraction. This attaches to a pair of sturdy stands with countersunk lag screws and washers. The bench simply clamps to your primary bench and includes a quick-release vise and holes for bench dogs and hold-downs.

**FIGURE 1**
Auxiliary Workbench

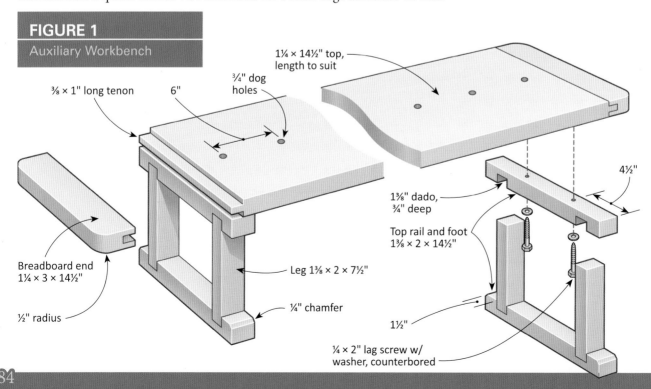

⅜ × 1" long tenon

6"

¾" dog holes

1¼ × 14½" top, length to suit

4½"

1⅜" dado, ¾" deep

Top rail and foot 1⅜ × 2 × 14½"

Breadboard end 1¼ × 3 × 14½"

½" radius

Leg 1⅜ × 2 × 7½"

¼" chamfer

1½"

¼ × 2" lag screw w/ washer, counterbored

# CHAPTER 5

# DESIGNS FOR SHOP EFFICIENCY

## Sawhorse Roundup
Corral one or more of these sturdy work supports for your shop.

Regardless of your shop's size, you can hardly call it complete without a few trusty steeds. A pair of horses can help support work for hand-sawing and machining, supply legs for an assembly table, or create an instant workstation. We designed three variations, each with special benefits so you can choose the one that best serves your needs.

We begin with a simple *folding sawhorse* having two frames that hinge together at the top and at the bottom via a pair of hinged braces. Lightweight, this style collapses flat for easy transporting or storing and sets up in a jiffy, making it ideal for jobsite work.

The *carpenter's sawhorse*, our stoutest, features a low profile (at 24" high) that helps you perform a multitude of tasks, from hand-sawing to supporting heavy loads. A built-in shelf offers a place to store items you want close at hand. And while it has a wide permanent footprint, you can stack one atop the other to conserve valuable floor space. The beam can also serve as a clamping surface or as an ever-ready seat.

The last horse is sleek and simple. This *knockdown sawhorse* is light, easy to move, and has a modest footprint. The upright design lets you position a pair close together for small jobs or nestle them together when you stow them away. Add spacers to the top rail for use as a portable infeed/outfeed stand for stationary machines. If space is tight, the knockdown hardware makes them easy to disassemble.

OVERALL DIMENSIONS | 35"w × 15½"d × 24"h     32"w × 21"d × 31"h     28"w × 18"d × 32"h

## Folding Sawhorse

**1** Rip enough 2½"-wide material for top rails (A), bottom rails (B), legs (C), and braces (D) from ¾" stock. Referring to the **Cut List**, crosscut each piece to the final length.

**2** Mark the dadoes and rabbets on the faces and edges of top rails (A), bottom rails (B), and legs (C) (**Figure 1**). Install a dado set in your tablesaw and raise it to ¼". Using your miter gauge with an extension fence and tablesaw fence with a stopblock, cut all of the dadoes and rabbets on these parts, adjusting the fence and stopblock as needed. Dry-fit the parts.

**3** Align and adhere the top rails (A) together with double-faced tape. Now mark the handhold notch along the bottom edge of upper top rail. Jigsaw or bandsaw the notches out, cutting just outside the line. Use a spindle sander or drill-press drum sander to sand the ⅜"-radius corners to the line. Separate the parts.

Take the folding sawhorses anywhere you need work supports that set up fast.

**4** Glue and clamp the mating dadoes and rabbets making up the lap joints of the rail and leg frame assemblies (A/B/C). Check for square. Then sand smooth, easing the edges.

**5** Note the locations for the butt hinges on legs (C) where shown in **Figure 1** and install them. For the best results, use a self-centering bit to drill pilot holes, ensuring that the leaves are square to the legs. Now install the three lower hinges to braces (D) and attach them to bottom rails (B).

**NOTE:** Refer to the handy **Cut Lists** for each of these three horses: below, and on pages 88 and 90.

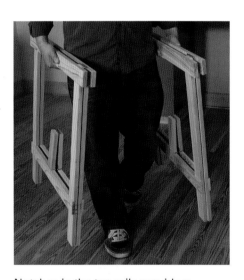

Notches in the top rails provide a handhold for easy toting.

### FIGURE 1
Folding Sawhorse
Exploded View

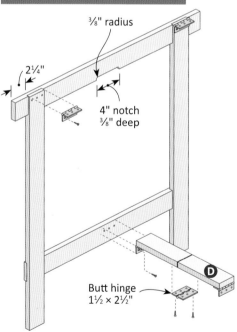

⅜" radius

2¼"

4" notch
⅜" deep

Butt hinge
1½ × 2½"

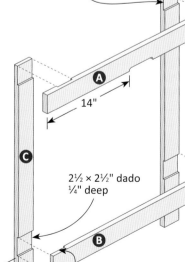

2½" × 2½" rabbet
¼" deep

14"

2½ × 2½" dado
¼" deep

6"

2½ × 2½" rabbet
¼" deep

## Folding Sawhorse Cut List

|   | PART | THICKNESS | WIDTH | LENGTH | QTY. | MAT'L |
|---|------|-----------|-------|--------|------|-------|
| A | Top rails | ¾" | 2½" | 32" | 2 | CP |
| B | Bottom rails | ¾" | 2½" | 27½" | 2 | CP |
| C | Legs | ¾" | 2½" | 32" | 4 | CP |
| D | Braces | ¾" | 2½" | 7⅛" | 2 | CP |

**Material:** CP=Cypress; **Hardware:** 1½ × 2½" butt hinges (5 needed)

The low profile of this sawhorse lets you pin workpieces with your knee. The lower tray serves as temporary tool storage.

## Carpenter's Workhorse

**1** Laminate two ¾ × 4 × 36" pieces to create the 1½"-thick workpiece. Now machine the piece to the sizes of the **Cut List** for beam (A). (A 2×4 also works.)

**2** Lay out the angled dado cut lines on the beam (A) for each leg (B), as shown in the **Angled Dado Detail** in **Figure 2** on page 88.

**3** To cut the angled dado on a tablesaw, you first need to make a wedge-like extension fence. Begin with a 15"-long piece of 2×4 and rip or joint off the rounded edges, making it 1½ × 3". Next, make a simple h-saddle for your saw fence from three pieces of MDF. Apply double-faced tape along the bottom edge of the saddle's face and adhere the 15"-long piece to it. Angle the blade at 14° and bevel-rip the piece as shown in **Photo A**, creating a wedge.

**4** Install a dado set and raise it ¾". Screw the wedge extension fence to your miter gauge, and angle the gauge at 10°. Place the top face of beam (A) against the fence, align the dado set with the cutlines, and cut the angled dado as shown in **Photo B**. Note that two of the angled dadoes for the legs will be cut from the left side of the dado set, and two from the right. Relocate and reposition the miter gauge to agree with the cutlines.

**5** Cut four legs to width and 2" longer than the dimensions in the **Cut List**. To avoid confusion, label the mating dadoes and legs 1-4. Fit one end of a leg (B) into one of the angled dadoes, and mark it along the inside face as shown in **Photo C** on page 88. Check the angle along the face; it should measure 10°. Now angle the blade at 14° and compound-cut the leg at one end. Mark parallel cutlines 25" from the cut ends of the legs and make the remaining compound cuts. (As an alternative, you can screw the legs in place proud, ensuring the horse stands level on the floor, and hand-cut the top ends flush with the beam.)

**6** Predrill and countersink holes through legs (B) and into the angled dadoes in beam (A). Next, apply glue and fasten each of the legs in place with three #8 × 1½" wood screws.

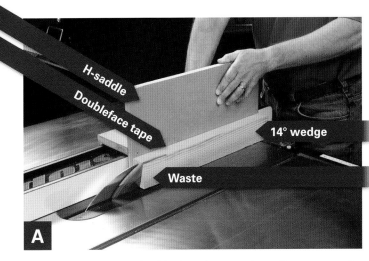

**A**

Use an h-saddle and double-faced tape to keep fingers out of harm's way when cutting the 14° wedge.

**B**

Clamp the beam to the wedge and cut at the angled dado cutlines. Now saw out the waste in between.

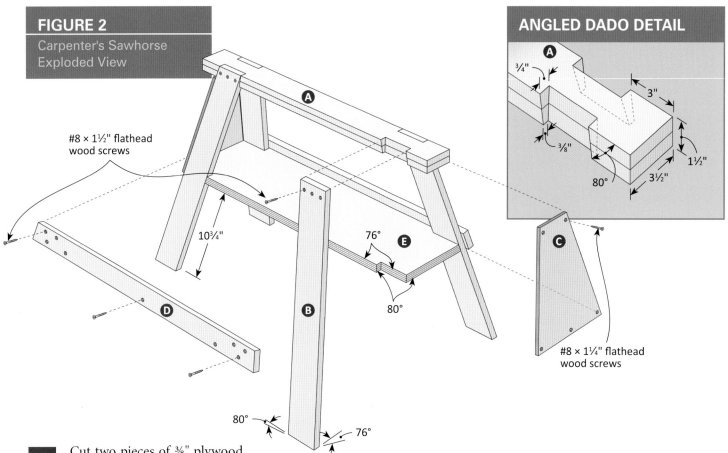

**FIGURE 2**
Carpenter's Sawhorse
Exploded View

**ANGLED DADO DETAIL**

Ⓐ
¾"
3"
⅜"
1½"
80°
3½"

#8 × 1½" flathead
wood screws

Ⓐ

10¾"

76° Ⓔ

80°

Ⓓ

Ⓑ

Ⓒ

#8 × 1¼" flathead
wood screws

80°

76°

**7** Cut two pieces of ⅜" plywood to the **Cut List** length for the trapezoidal gussets (C). For a precision fit, place the plywood at each end of the beam/legs assembly (A/B), and scribe along the outside edges of the legs onto the plywood. Use these lines to cut the tapering edges of the gussets on a bandsaw. Screw the gussets in place.

**8** Cut the stretchers (D) 2" longer than the **Cut List** dimension. Holding the pieces 10¾" up from the bottom ends of the legs (B), mark along the outside faces of the gussets (C) onto the inside faces of each stretcher for an exact fit. Angle-cut these pieces to final length and attach them with wood screws.

**9** Measure between gussets (C) and between stretchers (D) to see if the dimensions for the tool tray (E) check out. Adjust, if needed, and cut the part to size, bevel-cutting the edges at 14°. Mark and bevel-cut the corner notches with a bandsaw or jigsaw. Test-fit and screw it in place.

**NOTE**

Though the angle adjustments on the miter gauge and tablesaw blade for the compound cuts are for 10° and 14°, respectively, they correspond with the actual resulting angles on the parts shown in **Figure 2**.

**C**

With a leg slipped into an angled dado proud of the part's top face, pencil a cutline.

## Carpenter's Sawhorse Cut List

| | PART | THICKNESS | WIDTH | LENGTH | QTY. | MAT'L |
|---|---|---|---|---|---|---|
| A+ | Beam | 1½" | 3½" | 35" | 1 | CP |
| B* | Legs | ¾" | 3½" | 25" | 24 | CP |
| C* | Gussets | ⅜" | 9¾" | 12" | 2 | PLY |
| D* | Stretchers | ¾" | 2½" | 35" | 2 | CP |
| E* | Tool tray | ¾" | 2½" | 33½" | 1 | PLY |

**Material:** CP=Cypress; PLY=Plywood
+ Made from two pieces of laminated ¾" stock.
* Indicates parts are initially cut oversized. See instructions.

## Knockdown Trestle Horse

**1** Cut the legs (A) and feet (B) to the overall dimensions in the **Cut List** on page 90.

**2** Whether building one stand or a pair, align and adhere the legs (A) and feet (B) together in two stacks with double-faced tape. Referring to **Figure 3** on page 90, mark the tapers and notch on the leg stack. Set up the fence and a stopblock on the bandsaw, and gang-cut the notches on the top ends of the legs as shown in **Photo D**. Remove the fence and stopblock to bandsaw the tapered ends, cutting outside the lines. Sand to the lines using a stationary belt/disc sander. Similarly, mark, gang-cut, and sand the stack for feet (B), including the notch along the bottom edge. Use a spindle sander to sand the radii.

These stands rely on knockdown hardware for assembly. Make a pair for a work table; add a spacer to use one for an outfeed work support.

**3** Lay out the ¼" holes on the top face of the stack for legs (A). Then lay out the centers and ⅜" dowel holes on the bottom end of the stack for legs (A) and on the top edges of the stack for feet (B). Chuck a ¼" brad-point bit in your drill press, adjust the fence, and drill the holes through the leg stack. Separate the legs and feet in each stack.

**4** Using a self-centering doweling jig and stop on a ⅜" brad-point bit, drill the dowel holes in the ends of the legs (A) and feet (B) as shown in **Photo E**.

Nest the stands to save space or store the parts on the rack at left.

**D**

Bandsaw cuts along the notch cutlines, adjusting the fence as needed. Then make multiple cuts to remove the waste; clean up the notch with a chisel.

**Stopblock**

**E**

Clamp the workpiece in a bench vise, align the doweling jig with the centerline, and bore the holes to depth plus $^1/_{16}$" to make room for glue.

**5** Apply glue in the mating dowel holes for the legs (A) and feet (B), insert the dowels as shown in **Photo F**, and squeeze the parts together using bar clamps.

**6** Cut the top rail (C), lower rail (D), and spacers (E) to the sizes in the **Cut List**. Cut the notches in the top rails where shown. Now, mark and drill the holes in the ends of the lower rails using a doweling jig and guiding off the holes drilled in legs (A). Drill the cross dowel holes. Insert the connector bolts and cross dowels (**Photo G**), drop in the upper rails, and put your horses to work.

**FIGURE 3**
Knockdown Trestle Horse
Exploded View

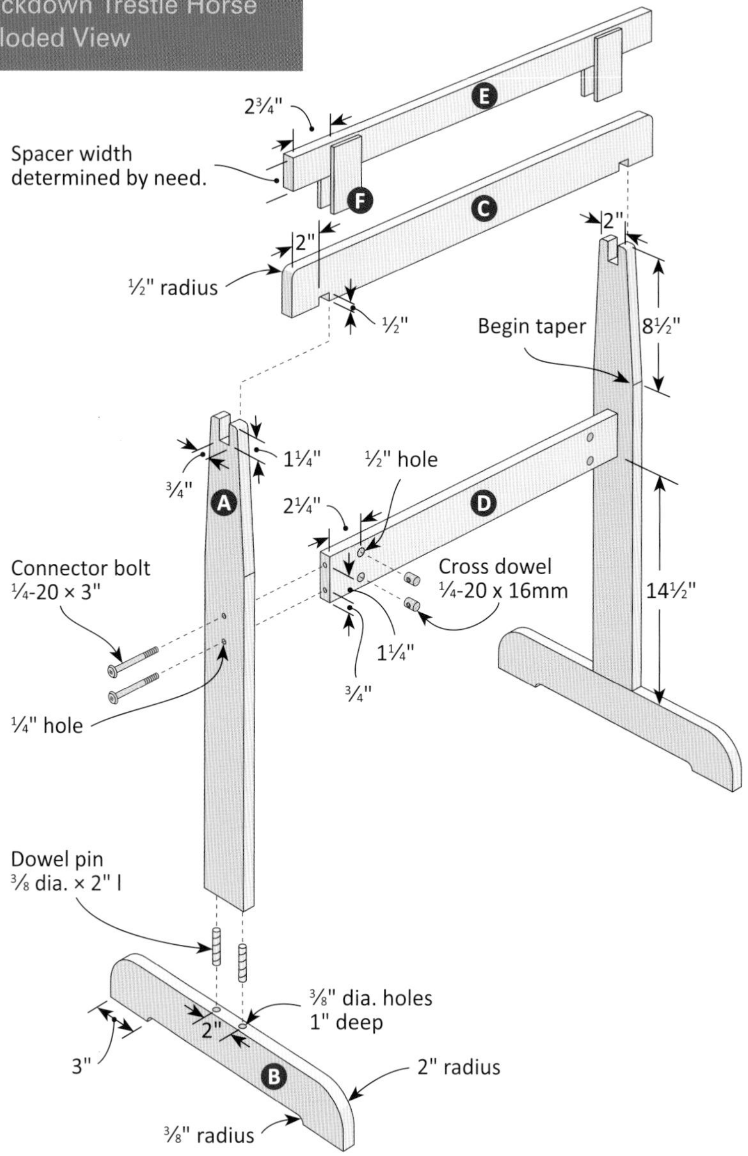

E
2¾"
Spacer width
determined by need.
F
C
2"
2"
½" radius
½"
Begin taper
8½"
1¼"
½" hole
¾"
A
2¼"
D
Connector bolt
¼-20 × 3"
Cross dowel
¼-20 x 16mm
14½"
1¼"
¾"
¼" hole
Dowel pin
⅜ dia. × 2" l
⅜" dia. holes
1" deep
2"
3"
B
2" radius
⅜" radius


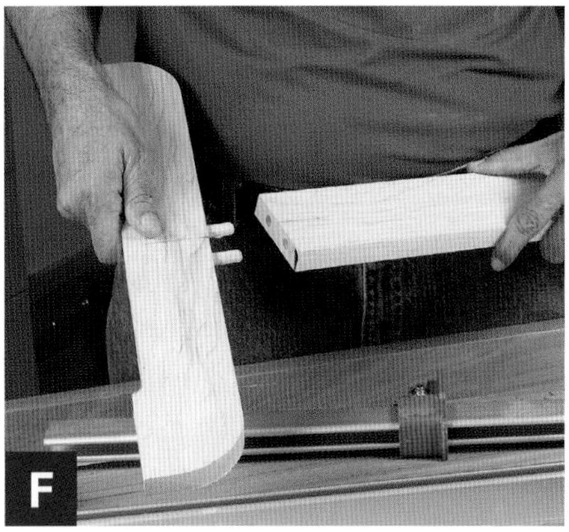

F


Spread glue in the holes, insert the dowels, and press the parts together with clamps.

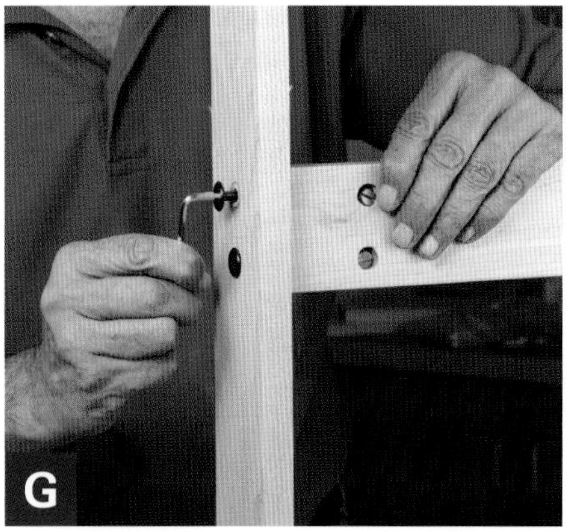

G


Use an Allen wrench to firmly tighten the leg/feet assemblies against the lower rail.

## Knockdown Trestle Horse Cut List

| | PART | THICKNESS | WIDTH | LENGTH | QTY. | MAT'L |
|---|---|---|---|---|---|---|
| A | Legs | ¾" | 3" | 28" | 2 | M |
| B | Feet | ¾" | 3" | 18" | 2 | M |
| C | Upper rail | ⅜" | 2¾" | 28" | 1 | M |
| D | Lower rail | ¾" | 2¾" | 22½" | 1 | M |
| E† | Spacer | ¾" | As needed | 28" | 1 | M |
| F† | Cleats | ¼" | 2" | 4" | 4 | PLY |

**Material:** M=Maple; PLY=Plywood
† Optional.

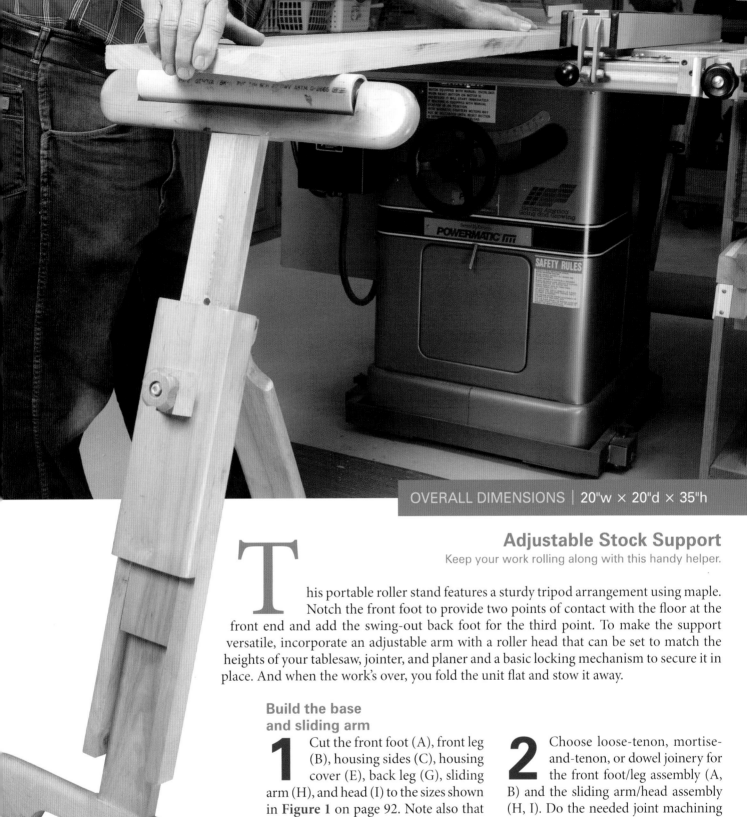

## Adjustable Stock Support

Keep your work rolling along with this handy helper.

This portable roller stand features a sturdy tripod arrangement using maple. Notch the front foot to provide two points of contact with the floor at the front end and add the swing-out back foot for the third point. To make the support versatile, incorporate an adjustable arm with a roller head that can be set to match the heights of your tablesaw, jointer, and planer and a basic locking mechanism to secure it in place. And when the work's over, you fold the unit flat and stow it away.

### Build the base and sliding arm

**1** Cut the front foot (A), front leg (B), housing sides (C), housing cover (E), back leg (G), sliding arm (H), and head (I) to the sizes shown in **Figure 1** on page 92. Note also that the bottom edge of the front foot is bevel-cut at 17°.

**2** Choose loose-tenon, mortise-and-tenon, or dowel joinery for the front foot/leg assembly (A, B) and the sliding arm/head assembly (H, I). Do the needed joint machining now, but hold off gluing the parts together. If going with loose tenons, rip and plane a 12"-long piece of tenon stock to ¼" thick by 1½" wide. Round-over the edges and test the stock's fit in the slot mortises. Sand, if needed, and then cut two 2"-long loose tenons. Set them aside.

**FIGURE 1**

Stock Support Exploded View

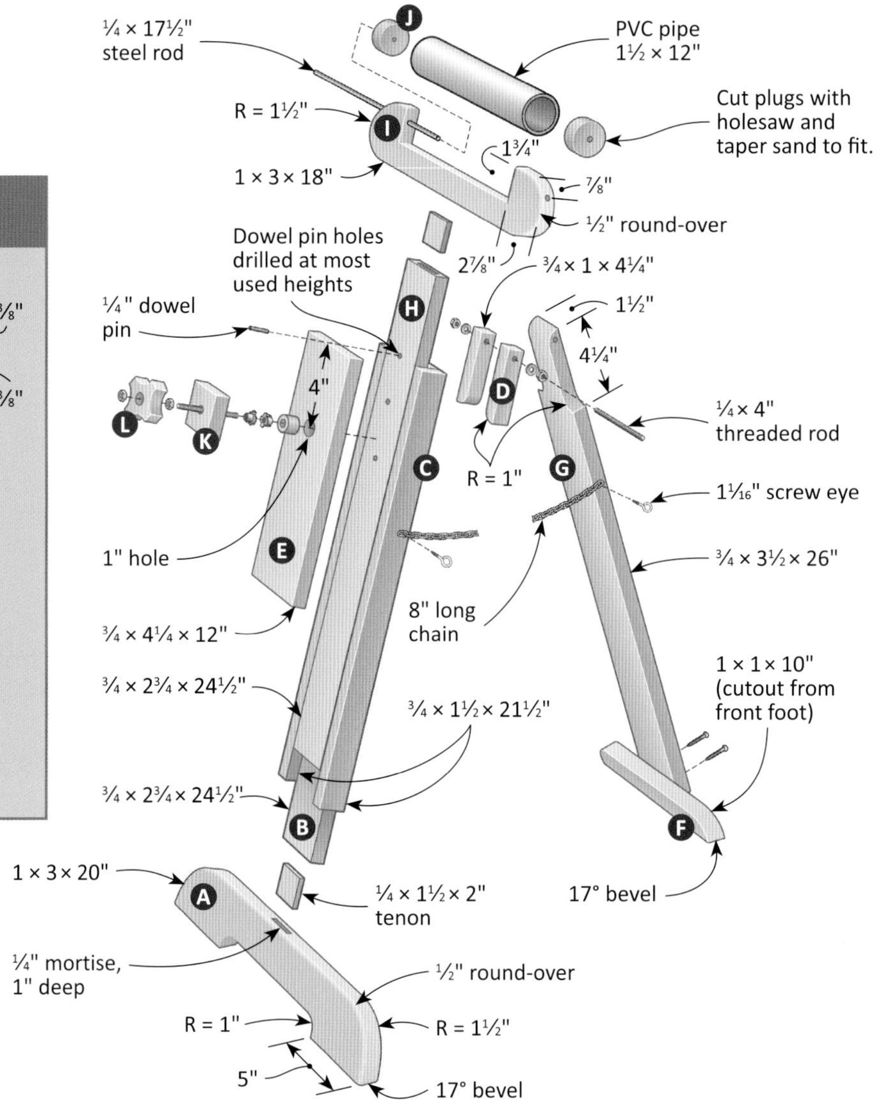

¼ × 17½" steel rod
PVC pipe 1½ × 12"
J
R = 1½"
I
Cut plugs with holesaw and taper sand to fit.
1¾"
1 × 3 × 18"
⅞"
½" round-over
Dowel pin holes drilled at most used heights
2⅞"
¾ × 1 × 4¼"
¼" dowel pin
H
1½"
4¼"
4"
D
¼ × 4" threaded rod
L
K
C
R = 1"
G
1¹⁄₁₆" screw eye
1" hole
E
¾ × 3½ × 26"
8" long chain
¾ × 4¼ × 12"
1 × 1 × 10" (cutout from front foot)
¾ × 2¾ × 24½"
¾ × 1½ × 21½"
¾ × 2¾ × 24½"
B
F
1 × 3 × 20"
A
¼ × 1½ × 2" tenon
17° bevel
¼" mortise, 1" deep
½" round-over
R = 1"
R = 1½"
5"
17° bevel


## LOCK SECTION VIEW

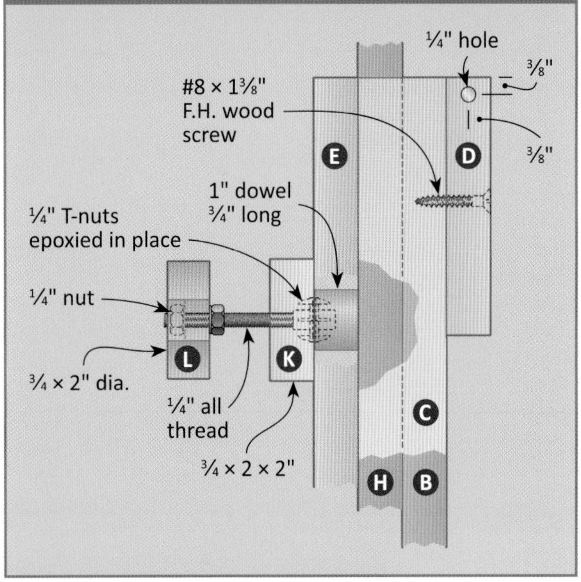

¼" hole
⅜"
#8 × 1⅜" F.H. wood screw
E
D
⅜"
1" dowel ¾" long
¼" T-nuts epoxied in place
¼" nut
L
K
¾ × 2" dia.
¼" all thread
C
¾ × 2 × 2"
H
B


## KNOB FRONT VIEW

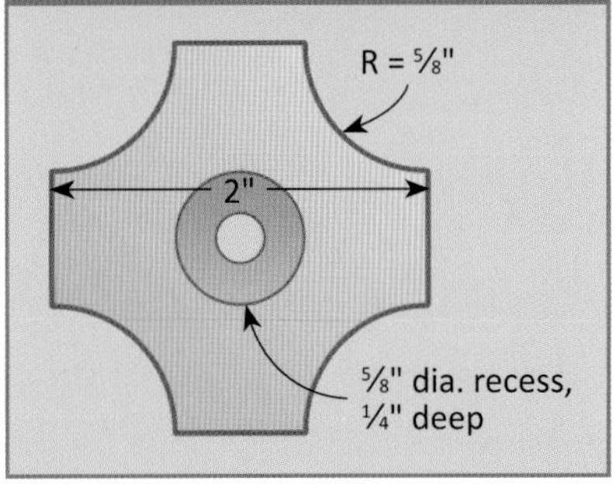

R = ⅝"
2"
⅝" dia. recess, ¼" deep


**3** Mark a centered hole ⅞" down from the top edge of head (I) on each end. Using a tall right-angle fence and clamps on the drill press to secure the workpiece, bore ¼" holes 3" deep into the ends for the ¼" steel rod. Also, drill the ¼" pivot hole through the top end of back leg (G), which includes brackets (D).

**4** Mark the radii on the front foot (A), back leg (G), and head (I). Strike a line between the radii on the bottom edge of the front foot to describe the notch. Bandsaw all the radii to shape and cut out the front foot notch, cutting just outside the lines. Note that when you cut the radii on the back leg and front foot that you cut out brackets (D) and back foot (F). Sand all radii to the cutlines. Sand a radius on the top inside end of the back leg to allow it to swing out.

**5** Install a dado set in your tablesaw and raise it to 1¾". Strike cutlines 2⅞" in from the ends of the head (I). Now, using a sacrificial extension fence on your miter gauge, cut out the roller assembly notch.

**6** Build the lock housing by first gluing and clamping the housing sides (C) to the front leg (B), flushing the sides' edges with the back of the leg. Let dry. Temporarily clamp the housing cover (E) to the assembly, and then plane and joint the sliding arm (H) until it slides smoothly in the housing. Drill the 1" hole in the housing cover, and then glue and clamp the cover in place.

**7** Glue and clamp the front foot (A) to the front leg (B) and the sliding arm (H) to the head (I). (We show loose tenon joinery.) Let dry. Center, glue, and screw the back foot (F) to the back leg (G).

**8** Rout ½" stopped round-overs along the ends and top edge of front foot (A) and ends and bottom edge of head (I).

## Shop Cart
Control clutter and speed production.

This cart was made for the express purpose of easily moving project parts between work stations for the next machining operation. No more will piles of wood and components be scattered hither and yon on your workbenches and saw tables.

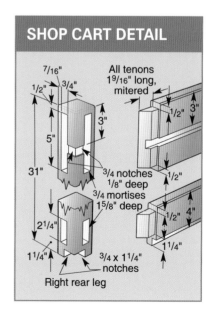

### FIGURE 1
Shop Cart

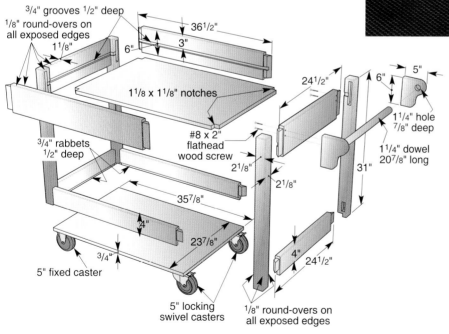

³/₄" grooves ¹/₂" deep
¹/₈" round-overs on all exposed edges
1¹/₈"
6"
36¹/₂"
3"
1¹/₈ x 1¹/₈" notches
24¹/₂"
6"
5"
1¹/₄" hole ⁷/₈" deep
³/₄" rabbets ¹/₂" deep
#8 x 2" flathead wood screw
2¹/₈"
2¹/₈"
1¹/₄" dowel 20⁷/₈" long
31"
35⁷/₈"
24"
23⁷/₈"
³/₄"
4"
24¹/₂"
5" fixed caster
5" locking swivel casters
¹/₈" round-overs on all exposed edges

### SHOP CART DETAIL

7/16"
All tenons 1⁹/₁₆" long, mitered
¹/₂"  ³/₄"
¹/₂"  3"
5"
3"
¹/₂"
31"
³/₄ notches ¹/₈" deep
¹/₂"
³/₄ mortises 1⁵/₈" deep
2¹/₄"
4"
1¹/₄"
1¹/₄"
³/₄ x 1¹/₄" notches
Right rear leg

# Plywood Scooter

### Go easy on your back.

To ease the transfer of sheet goods from storage to the shop, build this plywood scooter. The base is an 18"-long piece of scrap with a notch cut into it. Skateboard wheel assemblies are mounted underneath.

## FIGURE 1
### Plywood Scooter

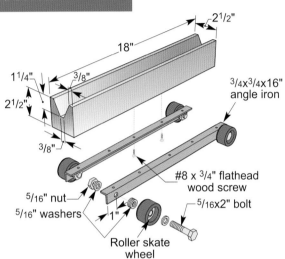

# Outrigger Roller

### Support long work for safer machining.

Because a drill-press table is not very large, a long piece of wood can shift or get out of level. To solve the problem, secure a small-diameter roller to a piece of scrap, and then clamp the scrap in a nearby vise to provide outfeed support.

## FIGURE 1
### Outrigger Roller

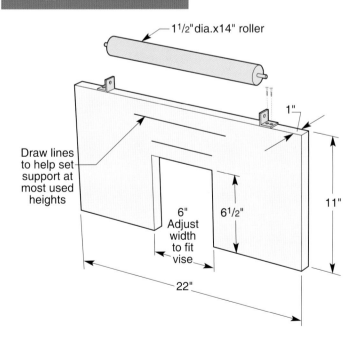